# CONTENTS

D0299917

## What is butter?

Butter is made from milk, which is first separated into cream and skimmed milk. The cream is used to make butter. It is churned by being moved around quickly in a special machine called a butter churner or continuous butter maker, until lumps of butter form (rather like when double cream is over-whipped). The butter is removed from the churn and packed.

Buttermilk and skimmed milk are the products left behind after butter has been made. They are the by-products of butter-making.

**Key to diagram**

Every day, tankers collect fresh milk from farms in the surrounding area.

Tankers unload their milk at the discharge bays, **A**, after a sample has been tested for quality. It is cooled at **C** and separated into cream and skimmed milk at **D**. The storage silos **B** are used to store milk prior to manufacture.

The cream is pasturized (heated) and cooled again and then aged in vats **E** before being churned into butter in the continuous butter-makers **F**.

The butter is automatically weighed and packed into boxes, **G**, and then stored in the cold store **H**, ready for distribution.

**I** is the creamery control room, **J** is the laboratory where milk and butter samples are tested, and **K** and **L** are storage silos for buttermilk and skimmed milk.

*Butter: the inside story. This is not an actual butter-making creamery but an artist's impression of the essential services in a modern plant*

# Structure

Butter is made up of:

▌fat

▌water

▌salt

▌protein

▌carbohydrate

▌fat-soluble vitamins
(A and D).

- 0.5% carbohydrate
- 0.5% protein
- 2% salt
- 16% water
- 81% fat

*The average composition of butter*

It is a mixture of liquid, crystals of fat and air bubbles. The type of butter (e.g. hard, soft, easily creamed) depends on:

▌the proportion of liquid fat to solid fat

▌the size of the fat crystals

▌the amount of air put in during manufacture.

The milk fat becomes either solid crystals of fat or 'free' fat, which is not in the form of crystals. If the crystals in the crystalline fat are evenly distributed and are all a similar shape and size then the butter tends to be crumbly and stiff in texture. If the non-crystalline, 'free' fat is irregular and unordered (i.e. randomly arranged) the butter melts more easily and has a smooth texture.

The yellow colour of butter comes from carotene. This comes from the food cows eat. Cows fed on grass get more carotene than those fed on cereals.

crystalline fat

free fat

air

water, milk and protein

*The microscopic structure of butter*

# Quality

**There are two types of butter:**

1  sweet cream butter (where the fat globules in cream are hardened by chilling before churning. They then churn easily into butter)
2  lactic butter (bacteria that produce lactic acid are added to the cream to start the process).

Each type of butter has a characteristic flavour. Both sweet cream butters and lactic butters can be bought salted (i.e. salt is added during production) and unsalted.

# Fact file

### *Lactic and sweet cream butters*

As the flavour of lactic and sweet cream butter is very distinctive, different countries favour making either the sweet cream or the lactic type.

For example:

UK, Australia and New Zealand butter is a sweet cream type

Denmark and other Scandinavian countries, Holland and France make lactic butter.

# Health and safety

▌The composition, labelling and advertisement of butter are controlled by law. The Butter Regulation 1966 (Statutory Instrument 1074) states that butter must contain:
  ◆not less than 80% milk fat
  ◆not more than 16% water
  ◆not more than 2% milk fat solids.

▌Butter must be kept cool, away from light and away from strong smelling and highly flavoured foods.

▌Light conditions and air can spoil the butter by:
  **a** making it go rancid (this happens because oxygen in the air changes some of the fat in the butter into a different substance with an 'off' taste)
  **b** reducing the amount of vitamin A in the butter. Some butter is sold in foil-lined packaging to protect it from light, air, flavours and odours.

▌Butter will keep for up to six weeks in a fridge and for six to nine months in a freezer.

# Nutritional value

## The nutritional value of butter (per 100 g)

The energy value of butter is what consumers consider most. Butter contributes on average about 15% of most people's total fat intake (as well as 13% of total vitamin A intake and 5% of total vitamin D intake). The following figures show the energy value of three different-sized servings of butter:

| | |
|---|---|
| The amount usually used to spread thinly on bread (7 g) | 212 kJ |
| A small single-portion pack of butter (usually 10 g) | 303 |
| The average size portion of butter used in a jacket potato (20 g) | 606 |

| | | |
|---|---|---|
| Energy | 731 kcal<br>30,031 kJ | Kilocalories<br>Kilojoules |
| Protein | 0.5 g | |
| Fat | 81 g | |
| Water | 16 g | Grams |
| Calcium | 15 mg | Milligrams |
| Vitamin A | 995 µg | |
| Vitamin D | 1.25 µg | Micrograms |

# Functional properties

▶ Butter can improve and add to the flavour and appearance of other ingredients and products.

- ◆ It brings out (enhances) the natural flavour of some foods, such as vegetables, fish, poultry, etc.
- ◆ It adds to the taste of baked foods such as cakes, biscuits, pastry, etc. because of its unique and appealing flavour.
- ◆ It improves the appearance of some foods because it produces a shiny glaze if used on the surface, as in grilling, frying, etc.
- ◆ When bread is buttered for sandwiches the butter separates the filling from the bread. It prevents the sandwiches from being soggy because the bread cannot easily absorb moisture from the filling. It provides 'protection' between the filling and the bread.

▶ The high temperature at which butter melts (36–40°C) is a useful property when making sauces, fillings and baked products, where a fat with a high **melting point** is required.

▶ The water in butter begins to foam, spit and separate from the fat at temperatures above 100°C. Above 121°C the **smoke point** of butter is reached. This is the stage at which the butter breaks up into gas and sediment. The gas is the water evaporating and the sediment is the proteins. As the temperature rises the sediment goes brown and smoky fumes are given off. (This is because a substance in the butter called glycerol is changed into acrolein which smells acrid, irritates the nose and eyes, and produces an unpleasant flavour.) If butter is to be used for sautéing or shallow frying it needs to be clarified before use, or a tablespoon of oil added to it to increase the temperature at which the smoke point is reached. This is because the temperature range needed for shallow frying most foods is between 177°C and 190°C.

Butter is clarified by:
- heating it gently until it foams
- continuing to heat it gently until the foam disappears and then removing it from heat
- waiting until the solid pieces have sunk to the bottom
- straining it to remove the solid pieces.
  The strained liquid is clarified butter, which can be used for all shallow frying methods. Ghee is Indian clarified butter, sometimes made from buffalo milk.

*Butter can improve and add to the flavour and appearance of other products or can be combined with other ingredients to make many varieties of products*

Butter shares other functional properties with other fats and oils. These are covered on pages 22–5.

## Combining butter with other ingredients

When butter is combined with other ingredients in flour mixtures (e.g. for scones, cakes, etc.) it melts easily and separates the other ingredients to create an open texture and good 'crumb'.

When butter is combined with ingredients to make pastries, such as rough puff pastry, it makes smooth layers between the layers of dough, which melt easily and help to produce a light crisp product. The melted butter is absorbed by the dough.

Butter can be combined with herbs, etc. to make a flavoured butter.

It can be combined with fish, minced chicken, etc. to make a well-flavoured 'set' pâté.

## Recipe

### Shortbread

1 teaspoon cooking oil
110 g softened (but not liquid) butter
50 g caster sugar
175 g plain flour
2 tablespoons caster sugar

Grease a baking tray with the cooking oil, using a pastry brush.
Heat oven to 150°C 300°F, gas mark 2.
Put the butter into a mixing bowl and beat until soft.

Beat in the 50 g of sugar and then the flour. Press together to make a paste.
Roll the paste out to 1 cm thickness on a sugared surface (use one tablespoon of caster sugar for this).
Cut the biscuits out using a 7.5 cm cutter.
Bake for about 25–30 minutes until golden brown.
Remove from the oven. Dust with the remaining caster sugar. Cool on a cooling tray.

# 2 CEREALS

## What are cereals?

▶ Cereals are the grain or seeds of cultivated grasses.

▶ The main cereals are:

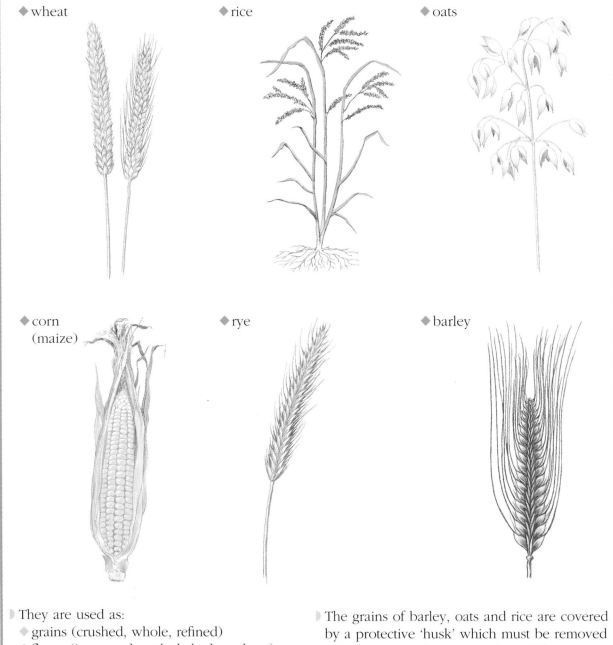

◆ wheat

◆ rice

◆ oats

◆ corn (maize)

◆ rye

◆ barley

▶ They are used as:
  ◆ grains (crushed, whole, refined)
  ◆ flours (in pasta, breads, baked products)
  ◆ breakfast cereals.

▶ The grains of barley, oats and rice are covered by a protective 'husk' which must be removed before they can be used as food. Wheat, corn and rye do not have this protective husk.

## Structure

## Wheat

▍All cereal grains have a similar structure. Wheat is looked at in detail here because it is the most used cereal in the UK. For other cereals see pages 14–15.

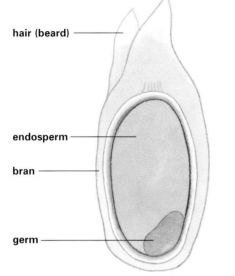

hair (beard)

endosperm

bran

germ

*A grain of wheat cut lengthwise*

◆ The endosperm contains starch and proteins.
◆ The germ or embryo is where a new plant will begin.
◆ The bran is the outside layer which covers the grain.

▍There are different varieties of wheat. 'Strong' wheats have a high protein content. 'Weak' wheats have less protein.

▍Wheat is milled to make flour. Some wheats mill more easily than others. Hard wheats have an endosperm which separates easily from the bran without breaking during milling. The endosperm of soft wheats does not separate easily and breaks during milling.

### Wheat flour

▍Flours are classified according to:
  **a** how much and which parts of the grain are used
  **b** the type of wheat used.

▍The percentage of the grain used in the flour is called the extraction. The milling process can produce flours with different extraction rates.

▍White flour has an extraction rate of about 72%. (The 28% *not* used is the bran and the wheatgerm.)

▍Wholemeal flour has an extraction rate of between 80 and 90%. (The 10–20% removed is the coarser bran.)

▍Wheatgerm flour is made from white flour which has 10% by weight of finely ground wheatgerm added to it.

▍Hard wheat produces strong flour with a higher protein content. The wheat proteins are called gliadins and glutenins. When water is added to flour (i.e. when it is 'hydrated') the two proteins join together and make a stretchy, elastic substance called **gluten**.

▍Soft wheat produces 'soft' flour with less protein.

▍All flour contains between 70–80% starch and about 2% sugar in the form of maltose.

▍White flour has a trace of fat only. By law it has to have iron, thiamin and nicotinic acid added during production to replace what is removed in the milling process.

▍Some flour contains improvers, which whiten it and make it perform better in cooking. They include ascorbic acid, potassium bromide, ammonium or potassium persulphate, and ammonium chloride.

*There are many different types of wheat flour*

### Different flours suit different mixtures and cooking processes.

- Plain white flours are medium strength. They contain about 10% protein. They do not contain a raising agent. They are ideal for shortcrust pastries, cakes (provided a raising agent is added) and biscuits.

- Strong flours have a high protein content (up to 17%) and are ideal for mixtures that must have elastic, stretchy dough, such as bread, pasta and flaky pastries. They can be white or 'brown'.

- Granary flour is a mixture of white flour and rye flour, with whole grains and malt extract added.

- Self-raising flours are medium-soft flours with chemical **raising agents** added (sodium bicarbonate and either acid calcium phosphate or acid sodium pyrophosphate).

The amount of raising agent added is:
- the right amount for cakes such as Victoria sponge sandwich
- not enough for plain (i.e. low-fat) mixtures, such as scones
- too much for 'rich' mixtures with a lot of egg and/or fat in them.

- Soft or cake flour has a low protein content (about 8%) and produces a melt-in-the-mouth texture. It is ideal for biscuits and cakes, particularly 'rich' ones.

*Different flours are used for different products and cooking methods*

## Nutritional value

**The nutritional value of white flour and bread and wholemeal flour and bread (per 100 g)**

| | White flour | White bread | Wholemeal flour | Wholemeal bread | |
|---|---|---|---|---|---|
| Energy | 348 kcal 1483 kJ | 251 kcal 1068 kJ | 318 kcal 1351 kJ | 241 kcal 1025 kJ | Kilocalories Kilojoules |
| Protein | 10 g | 8 g | 13.2 g | 9.6 g | |
| Fat | 0.9 g | 1.7 g | 2 g | 31 g | |
| Carbohydrate | 80 g | 54.3 g | 65.8 g | 46.7 g | |
| Water | 13 g | 39 g | 14 g | 38 g | Grams |
| Calcium | 138 mg | 100 mg | 65 mg | 28 mg | |
| Iron | 2.1 mg | 1.7 mg | 4 mg | 3 mg | |
| Thiamin | 0.3 mg | 0.18 mg | 0.46 mg | 0.24 mg | |
| Riboflavin | 0.03 mg | 0.03 mg | 0.08 mg | 0.09 mg | |
| Nicotinic acid equivalent | 2.7 mg | 2.6 mg | 5.6 mg | 1.9 mg | Milligrams |

- Flour and bread are good sources of energy. They also supply protein in the diet. For example, average consumption of bread supplies about 14% of the daily amount of protein recommended for most people (called the Reference Nutrient Intake, or RNI). The recommendations on dietary requirements are detailed in the COMA (Committee on Medical Aspects of Food Policy) report of 1991 along with other dietary reference values (DRVs).

- The amount of non-starch polysaccharides (NSP), or dietary fibre, is higher in flour with a high extraction rate.

**Dietary fibre in three types of bread (per 100 g)**

| | |
|---|---|
| white bread | 2.7 g |
| brown bread | 5.1 g |
| wholemeal bread | 8.5 g |

## Health and safety

- Flour is perishable. It must be kept dry and is best stored in a cool and airy place. Bags of flour are best kept in a tin or storage jar with a tight-fitting lid.

- Check the 'use by' date on the bag before using the flour.
- New flour should not be added to older flour for storage. The older flour must be used first.

## Functional properties of flour

### Gluten

- Gluten is produced when water is added to the proteins, gliadins and glutenins. Strong flour produces the most gluten.

- Gluten stretches easily, and becomes more elastic, stronger and smoother the more it is 'worked' (e.g. rolling the dough for flaky pastry or kneading a bread dough). The gluten in strong flour is more stretchy and elastic than in other flours.

- Fat and sugar reduce the strength of gluten.

### *The effect of heat*

- When dough is heated, the gluten 'network' is stretched by bubbles of gas produced in the dough by raising agents (e.g. yeast). These bubbles of gas are like small balloons and make the bread or other product 'rise'.

- The gluten proteins coagulate (i.e. become more solid) in the heat to produce a stable 'risen' product.

### Starch

### *Gelatinization*

- Starch does not dissolve in water until heat is applied. At about 60°C the starch granules begin to absorb water.

- At about 85°C the granules have absorbed about five times their volume of water.

- Eventually so much water is absorbed that the granules swell and make a paste with the water. This paste is called a **gel** and the process is called gelatinization.

- Further heating will make sure that all the granules have swollen and total gelatinization has taken place. If this doesn't happen the product will have a grainy texture and an uncooked starchy flavour.

- When starch gelatinizes it helps to produce moist baked products with a good texture and volume. The starch grains absorb moisture from the dough (e.g. for bread, cakes, pastries) and as the temperature rises during baking they gelatinize.

- Gelatinization of starch is also used to thicken sauces, soups, etc.

- Acids affect gelatinization, so, for example, an acid ingredient, such as tomatoes in tomato soup, can make the soup become thin if it is left standing.

- Chilling and freezing can cause a mixture thickened by flour starch to 'weep'. The moisture leaks out on thawing and the gel breaks up. This is because the gel 'tightens' when frozen and the liquid is squeezed out. This is called **retrogradation**. This will not happen if another type of starch is used for thickening, e.g. from cornflour or potatoes.

### *Browning*

- Starch helps baked products to become brown. As the temperature rises the starch turns brown. It gives bread and other baked products a golden brown colour. Brown sauces can be made by cooking a 'roux' – a mixture of fat and flour – until it turns brown. If heated too much the browning goes too far and the product becomes charred (burnt).

## Combining flour with other ingredients

- Flour can be combined with a variety of ingredients to make many very different products.

- The characteristics of these products depend on:
  - the other ingredients – e.g. flour is combined with: fat, yeast and liquid to produce bread; fat, flavouring and liquid to produce sauces, gravies etc; fat and liquid to produce pastries; fat, sugar, eggs and liquid to produce cakes
  - the proportion in which the other ingredients are used – e.g. in shortcrust pastries, half the amount of fat to flour is used whereas in flaky pastries two-thirds to three-quarters the amount of fat to flour is used
  - the methods of preparation and cooking used – e.g. a pancake batter (where a large proportion of liquid to flour is used) is fried, whereas a creamed pudding mixture can be steamed or baked.

### Pasta

Pasta is made from stong wheat, called durum wheat, combined with water. The milling of the wheat produces semolina, which is the coarsest grade of the starchy endosperm. Water is added to make the pasta. The gluten network in the pasta is very strong and is able to stand up to the processes of **extrusion** – to make strands of penne, macaroni, spaghetti – and **moulding** – to make shapes, such as fusilli (twists), fiochetti (bows), lasagne, conchiglie (shells), etc.

*Just a few of the many varieties of pasta*

## Combining pasta with other ingredients

- There are many different ingredients that combine well with pasta to make dishes and products. For example:
  - ravioli – where two sheets of pasta surround a flavoured mixture (e.g. ricotta cheese and spinach). The 'sandwich' is then cut into shapes, usually squares. The squares are simmered in water or stock and served with a sauce or sprinkled with cheese
  - spaghetti bolognese – a rich meat and tomato sauce mixed into cooked spaghetti.

- There are many advantages to combining pasta and other ingredients:
  - flavour, moisture and variety are added
  - a dish is made nutritionally more valuable because the combination of the protein in pasta and the protein from another ingredient such as beans or cheese provides all the indispensable **amino acids** the body needs. The proteins complement each other. This is called the complementary action of protein.

*Pasta can be combined with other ingredients*

# RICE

## What is rice?

- Rice is the grain of a cultivated grass.
- The grains are covered in a thick outer husk when harvested. This is removed during processing.
- Most types of rice are available as brown or white rice.
- White rice has the bran and germ removed and is sometimes polished to make it look shiny (pearly). It is made up of the starchy endosperm of the grain only.
- Brown rice has nothing other than the outer husk removed during processing. The bran and the germ are left on the grain. This increases the amount of dietary fibre the rice provides. It also increases the amount of time it takes to cook.
- Easy-cook rice has its starch partly gelatinized during processing. This makes the grains remain separate during cooking.

**There are different varieties of rice.**

- Short grain rice. These grains tend to 'clump' together when cooked. Pudding rice and Arborio rice (which is used for making risotto) are examples of short grain rice.
- Long grain rice. Carolina rice is a long grained variety. The grains remain fluffy, firm and separate when cooked, which makes it very popular. Basmati rice – a long, thin grain rice – is ideal to serve with Indian dishes, such as curry.

*white · long grain · short grain · easy cook · brown*

### Rice flour

This is a very finely ground flour which gives some mixtures a very 'short' texture when added to wheat flour (e.g. in shortbread). It can also be used to thicken soup, etc.

## Combining rice with other ingredients

- Rice has a high energy value. When it is combined with other ingredients (e.g. meat or vegetables) it is a valuable source of energy.
- It provides 'bite' and texture in a dish and soaks up liquid – for example, in rice pudding it absorbs the milk.
- It has a bland flavour which produces a 'balanced' taste when combined with strongly spiced food such as curry.

*Two very different uses for rice*

## Nutritional value

**The nutritional value of 100 g of rice compared with 100 g of spaghetti**

| | Rice | Spaghetti | |
|---|---|---|---|
| Energy | 359 kcal / 1531 kJ | 264 kcal / 1549 kJ | Kilocalories / Kilojoules |
| Protein | 6.2 g | 9.9 g | |
| Fat | 1 g | 1 g | |
| Carbohydrate | 86.8 g | 84 g | |
| Water | 13 g | 12 g | Grams |
| Calcium | 4 mg | 23 mg | |
| Iron | 0.4 mg | 1.2 mg | |
| Thiamin | 0.08 mg | 0.09 mg | |
| Riboflavin | 0.03 mg | 0.06 mg | |
| Nicotinic acid equivalent | 1.5 mg | 1.8 mg | Milligrams |

# OTHER WHEAT PRODUCTS

## Couscous

▌ These are tiny pellets of cereal made from semolina. They are used in North Africa to make a dish called couscous. Couscous cereal is best combined with flavouring ingredients, such as spices, herbs, onions, etc. to make a tasty dish. The pellets are mixed with water, which they absorb to produce moist separate grains ready for eating.

## Cracked wheat (bulgur)

▌ This is eaten a great deal in the Middle East. It is becoming popular in the UK.

▌ Wheat grains are boiled, dried and then ground to make bulgur. It is used in pilaff-type savoury dishes or soaked and served raw as a salad, such as tabbouleh.

## Noodles

▌ Noodles are made from flour, water and eggs. They are sometimes referred to as vermicelli. European noodles are mostly ribbon shaped.

▌ Asian noodles are sometimes made with flour from buckwheat, chick peas, mung beans as well as durum wheat. They are often sold in skeins (bundles) of fine threads.

noodles

bulgur

couscous

# OTHER CEREALS

## Oats

▌ These can be milled and processed to produce a variety of products e.g. muesli, rolled oats to make porridge, etc. Oats can also be combined with sugar and fat to make biscuits, etc. (e.g. flapjacks).

▌ Ground oatmeal is combined with other ingredients to make cakes, digestive biscuits, haggis (a Scottish dish of sheep's or calf's offal, suet and oatmeal).

## Rye

▌ This can be milled to produce flour. The flour has a low protein content and therefore produces a weak gluten structure in dough. It makes close textured, flat baked foods such as the German black bread called pumpernickel. It is also used to make crispbreads, such as Ryvita.

▌ To increase the strength of the flour it is sometimes combined with wheat flour to make rye bread.

# Barley

▶ This has a low protein content which means that little or no gluten is produced therefore it is not used to make flour.

▶ The husked, polished barley is called pearl barley. It is used in soups, stews and barley water.

# Corn (maize)

▶ This is used as a vegetable (e.g. corn-on-the-cob, corn nibbles/kernels), as flour and to make breakfast cereals such as cornflakes.

▶ The flour is called cornflour. It is made up entirely of the starch from maize because all the protein and fat are washed away during processing. Custard and blancmange powders are flavoured cornflour.

▶ Polenta is made from ground Indian corn. The paste made from it is low in gluten, so sometimes wheat flour and baking powder are added to make a lighter product. Flavourings are usually added to the paste, which is then cooked in various ways to serve as an accompaniment to meat, fish and vegetable dishes.

**The following ingredients are similar to cereal products, but they are not cereals.**

# Sago

▶ This is dried starchy granules from the sago palm. It is usually combined with milk and sugar to make puddings.

# Tapioca

▶ This is made of starch grains from flour made from the cassava plant. It too, is usually combined with milk and sugar to make puddings.

▶ Tapioca starch can also be used to thicken soups and stews.

# Arrowroot

▶ This comes from a West Indian plant called maranta. It is ground into a fine flour. It is almost all starch and is used to thicken mixtures such as sauces and stews. When gelatinized it becomes translucent (i.e. clear).

*Products made from oats, rye, barley and maize*

*Sago, tapioca and arrowroot are similar to cereals*

# Recipe for pesto

50 g fresh basil leaves
2 garlic cloves    25 g pine nuts
25 g finely grated parmesan cheese
2 tablespoons olive oil

Liquidize all ingredients except the olive oil. Drizzle in the olive oil. Purée until a smooth paste forms.
Store in the refrigerator until required.

# 3 CHEESE

## What is cheese?

Cheese is a solid or semi-solid form of milk. Most cheese is made from cow's milk. Sheep, goat, buffalo and reindeer milk is also used.

| Types of cheese | Examples |
|---|---|
| Hard pressed cheese | Cheddar, Lancashire and Cheshire |
| Soft cheese | Brie and Camembert |
| Blue veined cheese | Stilton, Gorgonzola, Danish Blue and Roquefort |
| Unripened cheese | Cottage cheese and cream cheeses |
| Processed cheese | Cheese spreads and cheese slices. (These are products made from other cheeses, often hard ones like Cheddar.) |

### Hard pressed cheese

▶ Eight pints of full cream milk are needed to make a pound of hard pressed cheese such as Cheddar. The flow chart shows how Cheddar is made.

| Milk | |
|---|---|
| Pasteurization | |
| Starter added | *This is a culture of special bacteria which turns the milk sour.* |
| Rennet added | *Rennet clots the milk by separating the curds and whey.* |
| Curd cut | *The whey drains away.* |
| Solid curd cut into strips/chips (Cheddaring) | *Strips/chips are washed to remove the whey. Drained and dried curds become 'silky' and more acid.* |
| Salting | *Salt is added for flavour and to preserve the cheese.* |
| Pressing and wrapping | *The cheese is packed into moulds ('hoops') and pressed to remove any remaining whey. Then it is wrapped by coating it with wax to make a rind. The rind stops the cheese from losing too much water, which would make it dry.* |
| Ripening (may take months or years depending on type of Cheddar) | *The action of bacteria and enzymes in the cheese develop the taste and texture of the finished cheese. The stronger the taste required the longer it takes. Ripening takes place between 5°C and 10°C.* |
| Grading | *A grader tests the cheeses and decides which will be eaten young and which will be kept to mature (to become stronger in flavour).* |
| Packing | *Different sizes are packed, e.g. large blocks or smaller pieces for retail sale. Some are vacuum packed for longer storage (this means that there is no air in the package).* |

## Soft cheese

▶ Made from fresh, not soured, milk.

▶ The curds are moister than hard cheese curds. The acidity develops a characteristic flavour as a result of moulds which grow on the outside. The moulds produce enzymes which break up the curds and soften the cheese from the outside inwards.

▶ Soft cheese is made in small flat shapes so that the inside ripens before the outside becomes spoilt.

## Blue veined cheese

▶ Made from medium-soft curds which are slowly drained from the whey. This makes more acid develop than in hard cheese.

▶ Mould is added to the cheese or it grows from the spores in the room used to ripen the cheese. The cheese is spiked or pricked to let oxygen and mould spores in. The mould grows gradually and spreads into the cheese. This makes the blue veins in the cheese.

## Unripened cheese

▶ Cream cheese is made from double cream, single cream or milk and cream mixed together.

▶ There are two methods for making cream cheese. Either rennet is added or the cream is soured to produce the curds.

▶ Salt is added for flavouring.

▶ Cottage cheese is made from pasteurised skimmed milk which, when cooled, is inoculated with a starter culture. Types of Lactococcus lactis are used as cultures.

## Processed cheese

▶ This is a mixture of cheeses which are grated, heated and have an emulsifying agent added. (This stops the cheese separating and makes a smooth product.)

▶ The cheese used is often a mixture of young and mature Cheddar.

▶ The mixed cheeses are melted and poured into moulds to harden. They are then sliced or packed into a variety of shapes such as blocks or individual portions. The cheese can also be made into a spread.

▶ Additional ingredients such as celery, ham, chives, etc. are sometimes added.

*Examples of the various types of cheese*

## Structure

Cheese is a curd, which contains most of the solids from milk (i.e. the protein, the fat and fat-soluble vitamins). Different cheeses have different amounts of each. The average percentage composition of four types of cheese is shown below.

| | Fat | Protein | Water |
|---|---|---|---|
| Hard cheese (e.g. Cheddar) | 35% | 25% | 37% |
| Soft cheese (e.g. Camembert) | 23% | 22% | 52% |
| Cream cheese (made with double cream) | 86% | 3% | 10% |
| Cottage cheese | 4% | 15% | 75% |

## Texture

**The texture of cheese varies. For example:**

▸ Cheddar and Double Gloucester cheeses are close textured.

▸ Lancashire, Caerphilly and Cheshire are 'crumbly'.

▸ Parmesan is very hard with a grainy texture. (In Italian it is known as Parmeggiano Reggiano, one of a group called *formaggi di grana* – 'grainy cheeses').

▸ Edam, a Dutch cheese, is semi-hard with a red wax coating.

▸ Mascarpone is an Italian cream cheese.

▸ Cottage cheese has small, individual curds.

▸ Quark (or quarg) is an 'acid' tasting cottage cheese.

▸ Fromage frais, rather like Quark, is sometimes whipped to make it soft, light and creamy in texture.

## Taste

**The taste of cheese also varies. For example:**

▸ Brie has a creamy fruity taste

▸ Cheddar has a 'mustardy' flavour, which can be mild through to very strong. Montery Jack, a type of Cheddar, has a bland, milky flavour; Cathedral City, another Cheddar, has a very strong, bitey/sharp flavour.

▸ Gruyère tastes milky.

▸ Caerphilly has a mild, slightly sour, taste.

## Strength

This refers to the 'depth' of flavour and its maturity. Much of the cheese sold in shops and supermarkets is identified by a number that relates to its maturity and depth of flavour. The blandest, mildest-flavoured cheeses are numbered 1 and the strongest 5 or 6.

*A supermarket cheese counter which indicates the strength of cheeses by giving them numbers*

## Nutritional value

### The nutritional value of various cheeses (per 100 g)

Cheese has a high energy value. Reduced/low fat varieties of most types are available and these have a lower energy value.

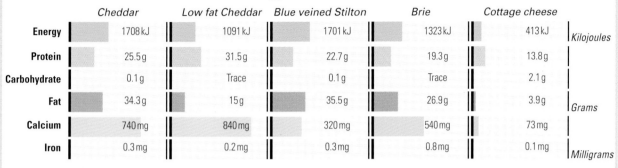

| | Cheddar | Low fat Cheddar | Blue veined Stilton | Brie | Cottage cheese | |
|---|---|---|---|---|---|---|
| Energy | 1708 kJ | 1091 kJ | 1701 kJ | 1323 kJ | 413 kJ | Kilojoules |
| Protein | 25.5 g | 31.5 g | 22.7 g | 19.3 g | 13.8 g | |
| Carbohydrate | 0.1 g | Trace | 0.1 g | Trace | 2.1 g | |
| Fat | 34.3 g | 15 g | 35.5 g | 26.9 g | 3.9 g | Grams |
| Calcium | 740 mg | 840 mg | 320 mg | 540 mg | 73 mg | |
| Iron | 0.3 mg | 0.2 mg | 0.3 mg | 0.8 mg | 0.1 mg | Milligrams |

## Extra facts

▶ **Casein** is the main protein in cheese. It contains all the indispensable **amino acids** in approximately the proportions that the human body needs.

▶ Cheese is a valuable source of easily absorbed calcium, vitamin A and riboflavin (vitamin B2).

▶ 100 g of grated cheese is about 10 level tablespoonfuls. About 45–50 g of grated cheese is needed to make a cheese sandwich. The nutritional value of this would be:

**45 g Cheddar**

| | | |
|---|---|---|
| Energy | 769 kJ | Kilojoules |
| Protein | 11.5 g | |
| Carbohydrate | 0.05 g | |
| Fat | 15.5 g | Grams |
| Calcium | 324 mg | |
| Iron | 0.1 mg | Milligrams |

▶ About 50 g of cottage cheese would be used as a sandwich filling. The nutritional value of this would be:

**50 g cottage cheese**

| | | |
|---|---|---|
| Energy | 207 kJ | Kilojoules |
| Protein | 6.9 g | |
| Carbohydrate | 1.1 g | |
| Fat | 2 g | Grams |
| Calcium | 36 mg | |
| Iron | 0.2 mg | Milligrams |

## Fact file

### More soft cheeses

Cottage cheese is the most popular unripened soft cheese in the UK. However, there are other unripened soft cheeses on the market which are increasing in popularity. They include cream cheese, quarg, and fromage frais.

Cream cheese has a slightly acidic flavour and is made from cream with a fat content of between 25–55 per cent. Many recipes for sweet cheese cakes state that cream cheese must be used.

Quarg is less well known. It is produced in large quantities in Europe. There are different varieties, the most popular being a fat free type. It has a smooth texture, is white in colour and has a mildly acidic rich flavour. It combines well with fruit and can be flavoured with herbs and spices in savoury dishes.

'Fresh cheese' is more usually labelled fromage frais. This is available in a number of forms. One popular variety is aerated (has air added) to give it a 'light', open consistency.

Cheese has a longer shelf-life than milk. The less moisture the cheese contains, the longer its shelf-life, so hard cheeses last longer than soft ones.

## Critical points

▶ All cheese should be covered and kept cool, preferably in a refrigerator. Cold cheese loses its flavour, so cheese should be removed from the fridge and kept for an hour at room temperature before eating.

▶ Soft cream cheeses and cottage cheeses must be stored in the refrigerator. They should be eaten within two to three days.

▶ Pre-packed cheese has a 'use by' or 'best before' date printed on the label, some also include a 'display until' date.

▶ Cheese that has been stored at too high a temperature 'weeps' and becomes oily on the surface. Warmth also makes mould form on the surface. This doesn't look nice and can alter the taste, but the cheese is safe to use when all mould is removed.

▶ Some cheese is labelled 'made with unpasteurized milk'. This is also known as raw milk (i.e. it has not been heat-treated). Pregnant women and other people who are vulnerable to infection should not eat this type of cheese.

Cheese is used in its natural state in a variety of ways. Its natural characteristics, such as texture, determine the best cheese for a particular purpose. For example:

▶ very hard cheese, such a Parmesan, grates finely and remains dry and in separate 'gratings'. This is ideal for sprinkling over salads, pasta dishes, etc.

▶ crumbly cheese such as Cheshire can be used in dressings, because it will mix in well with the dressing

▶ firm cheese that can be cut into cubes, such as Greek Feta, makes a good salad ingredient.

## The effects of cooking
**Cheese melts when it is heated. This is what happens:**

▶ The fat in the cheese separates from the protein. This happens at quite a low temperature, about 65°C. If it is heated gently at this temperature the cheese melts without losing all the fat.

▶ If the heat is too fierce two things happen:
   **a** all the fat is lost. It overcooks and smells bitter (acrid) – i.e. it decomposes
   **b** the protein becomes tough and hard because it has lost the layer of fat which coats and protects it.

**For successful results:**

▶ cheese should be heated gently for a short time

▶ a starchy food should be mixed with it, e.g. breadcrumbs. These absorb the fat

▶ cheese should be grated because it melts more easily and gives a smoother result

▶ the cheese chosen for a particular dish should have the characteristics the dish requires. For example, some cheeses that thread and become stringy when heated are the best for fondue. Emmenthal and Gruyère are examples. In a fondue the cheese is mixed with flavouring ingredients and heated, bread cubes are put onto forks, dipped into the mixture and coated with it before being eaten. This stringiness is caused by the **coagulation** (solidifying) of the casein (protein) and its separation from the fat

▶ processed cheese does not separate into melted fat and protein as easily as hard cheese because it takes longer for the fat to melt. This means that the protein doesn't become tough in the time it takes to cook processed cheese.

# Combining cheese with other ingredients

**The advantages of combining cheese with other ingredients are:**

- it increases the nutritional value of a dish (e.g. macaroni cheese, cheese on toast)
- it gives added flavour to a bland, mild-flavoured ingredient or dish (e.g. quiches or cauliflower in cheese sauce)
- it can be used to produce an attractive brown topping (e.g. in au gratin dishes)
- it introduces another flavour and texture (e.g. cheese and pineapple kebabs, cheese and apple pie, cheese and date sandwich filling)
- it allows a variety of sweet and savoury products to be made (e.g. cheese soufflé, cheesecake, cheesy dips).

*Cheese can be used in a variety of sweet and savoury dishes*

# Recipe

## Cheese soufflés

Sometimes called twice-baked soufflés, these can be made in advance.

Prepare four ramekins (150 ml size) by brushing with melted butter and pressing 15 g of grated Parmesan cheese on the bottom and sides of each.

$\frac{1}{2}$ small onion      2 bay leaves
small piece of carrot      225 ml milk
25 g unsalted butter      25 g plain flour
salt and pepper      2 eggs
120 g grated Cheddar cheese
1 heaped teaspoon dry mustard
100 g grated Parmesan cheese

Heat oven to 180°C 350°F, gas mark 4. Put the onions, bay leaves, carrot and milk in a saucepan. Bring to the boil. Melt the butter. Mix in the flour, salt and pepper. Cook for 30 seconds. Remove from heat.

Add the milk mixture gradually. Beat well. Return to the heat and bring to boil stirring all the time. Cool slightly.

Separate whites from yolks of the eggs. Beat the yolks into the sauce. Add the Cheddar cheese and mustard.

Whisk the egg whites to a soft peak. Fold into the sauce. Divide the mixture between the ramekins.

Put in a baking tin. Pour warm water into the tin to about 2 cms deep. Bake for 15–20 minutes. Remove from tin and refrigerate.

Heat oven to 200°C 400°F, gas mark 6. Loosen each soufflé and remove from the ramekins. Place bottom side up in an ovenproof dish.

Sprinkle 10 g Parmesan cheese on top of each. Bake for 20–25 minutes.

## What are fats and oils?

▶ The words 'fats' and 'oils' do not refer to different substances – they simply refer to the physical appearance (state) of the same type of substance. A fat that is liquid at normal room temperature is called an oil; one that is solid or semi-solid at normal room temperature is called a fat.

▶ Fats are made up of carbon, hydrogen and oxygen. They are links of fatty acids mixed with glycerol. Some fatty acids are **saturated**, which means that all the carbon is attached to hydrogen.

▶ Other fatty acids are **unsaturated**, which means that some of the carbon is not attached to hydrogen.

▶ The more saturated acids there are the harder the fat is. The more unsaturated acids there are the softer the fat is.

▶ Solid fats were originally produced as alternatives to lard. They include Trex, White Flora, etc.

## Structure

### Solid fats

▶ They are 99% fat.

▶ Some have gas added during manufacture which makes them remain soft over a wide range of temperatures – even at fridge temperature.

▶ They are of 'standard' consistency (i.e. they are always exactly the same, because they are manufactured to a precise specification).

▶ They have little or no flavour.

*A soya bean plant*

### Cooking oils

▶ They are 99.9% oil.

▶ They are lighter, more digestible and less greasy than solid fats.

▶ There are many types of cooking oils. For example:
  ◆ olive oil (strong flavour, low smoke poi – see page 25)
  ◆ corn oil, sunflower oil, ground nut oil (little flavour, high smoke point).

Most cooking oils such as ground nut oil a soya bean oil are produced from plants. Ground nut pods grow beneath the soil.

*The groundnut is a member of the pea and bean family. It buries its pods under the soil*

## Nutritional value

### Solid fats

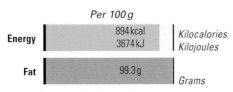

*Per 100 g*

| Energy | 894 kcal | Kilocalories |
| | 3674 kJ | Kilojoules |
| Fat | 99.3 g | Grams |

Manufactured fats often have a high proportion of unsaturated fats, because some vegetable oil is used to produce them.

### Cooking oils

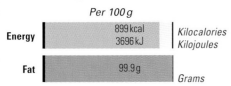

*Per 100 g*

| Energy | 899 kcal | Kilocalories |
| | 3696 kJ | Kilojoules |
| Fat | 99.9 g | Grams |

A high proportion of the fat in cooking oils is unsaturated because these products are made from vegetable oils such as sunflower oil.

*Most food shops and supermarkets stock many types and makes of fats and oils*

## Functional properties

### Foaming

▷ Fats such as soft margarines and butter will trap air bubbles when beaten or creamed and form a **foam**. The foam helps baked products such as Victoria sandwich cake to rise well and to have a light texture.

▷ Fats which produce successful foams have:
◆ a mouldable, pliable property called **plasticity**. This means that when the fat is creamed or beaten it is able to surround the air and make a large number of bubbles. This process is called **aeration**
◆ **emulsifying agents** which help the air bubbles to be evenly spread (dispersed) in the mixture
◆ some caster sugar added to help aeration (see page 77).

### Shortening

▷ Fats have a 'shortening' effect in pastry, shortbread and biscuit mixtures. This is how it happens:
◆ The fat coats the flour particles and reduces the amount of water which can mix with the flour (i.e. less water is absorbed).

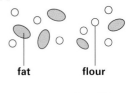

fat          flour

◆ The plasticity of the fat allows the fat to surround and coat the flour particles.

fat forming a waterproof coating around flour

◆ The 'shortening' effect produces a crumbly, melt-in-the-mouth texture. This happens because the proteins in flour make gluten when they are mixed with water. Gluten is elastic and stretchy.

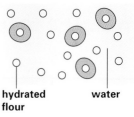

hydrated flour          water

When only a little water is absorbed by flour less gluten is produced and so the mixture is 'shortened'.

# Which are the best fats?

▌ Cooking fats that are almost all fat (e.g. lard and pure vegetable fats) are the best shortening agents. Fats that have plasticity are good because they surround the flour particles easily.

▌ Oils coat the flour particles almost completely which prevents almost all the water reaching the flour. This produces a very crumbly, dry texture, which is difficult to handle and almost impossible to roll out if pastry is being made.

# What else is important?

▌ The amount of fat to flour. There must be sufficient fat to reduce gluten development and not too much otherwise a 'greasy' product is made.

▌ The preparation method. The fat and flour must be thoroughly mixed in shortcrust pastry before the water is added.

▌ Fat can be used to produce a 'flaky', layered result. This is how:
 ◆ Layers of fat separate the layers of dough. This is particularly noticeable in flaky pastries.
 ◆ Air is trapped between the layers. Water in the dough turns to steam during cooking.
 ◆ The fat melts and is absorbed by the dough. This leaves empty spaces between the layers.
 ◆ The air and steam keep the layers separate, because:
  – the air expands in the heat and needs more room. It moves into the empty spaces
  – the steam is 'bigger' than the water from which it was made and, therefore, takes up more room. This 'pushes' the layers and empty spaces upwards.

## Stages in making flaky pastry

*A firm dough is made*

*After the dough has been rolled out, fat is dotted over two-thirds of it*

*The pastry is folded in three and rolled out again. Then the process is repeated*

# Other functions of fats

▶ Fats help to extend the shelf-life of baked products (e.g. bread and cakes) because they help the products to retain (keep) their moisture and therefore they do not dry out so quickly. Low fat mixtures such as scones dry out very quickly.

▶ Fat prevents 'lumps' of flour forming in sauces thickened with flour. The fat surrounds the flour particles and allows them to mix with the liquid to produce a smooth result.

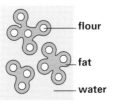

▶ Fat gives colour, flavour and 'shine' (glaze).

▶ Grilled and roasted food is prevented from drying when it is spread or basted with fat.

▶ Fat stops food sticking when the cooking container is greased.

▶ Fat allows food to be cooked by frying. The smoke point of fats is important here. A fat with a high smoke point is best. Above the smoke point:
   ◆ the oil or fat breaks down into a gas and sediment (it decomposes)
   ◆ a light blue smoke is given off
   ◆ an acrid smell and unpleasant flavour develop (see page 6).

Different fats have different smoke points, for example:

| Fat | Smoke point (approx.) |
|---|---|
| Unclarified butter | 121°C |
| Lard | 205°C |
| Most vegetable oils (but not olive oil) | 232°C |
| Vegetable 'shortenings' (these have added emulsifiers which lower the temperature of the smoke point) | 188°C |

*Fat is used for different purposes in different products*

## Recipe

### Vinaigrette dressing

1 tablespoon wine vinegar
salt and pepper
1 heaped teaspoon 'made' mustard (i.e. bought as a paste or made into a paste by adding water to the dry mustard powder)
150 ml olive oil (virgin is best)

Mix the vinegar, mustard, salt and pepper together.

Add the oil, little by little, beating well.

Store in a screw top jar (maximum time about a week).

Use as required.

# 5 CREAM

## What is cream?

▶ Cream is made from milk. The fat in the milk is separated from the rest of the milk. If you look at an unopened bottle of whole milk, you will see a yellowy layer on top – that is the cream. It floats to the top, because it is lighter than the rest of the milk.

▶ Some milk is **homogenized**. The fat globules are made very small and are evenly spaced throughout the milk. This means that the fat cannot be separated out, so this milk cannot be used for making cream.

▶ In large-scale cream production a machine is used to separate the fat from the milk. The diagrams on the right show how this is done.

The machine is called a centrifugal separator. The milk is spun round very fast. The watery skimmed milk is 'flung' to the outside and the fat (i.e. the cream) moves towards the centre because it is lighter. The cream then goes out through a pipe and is collected. The separator has a valve which is adjusted depending on what type of cream is required. This valve allows the amount of watery skimmed milk in the cream to vary according to whether double (full) cream or single cream is being produced.

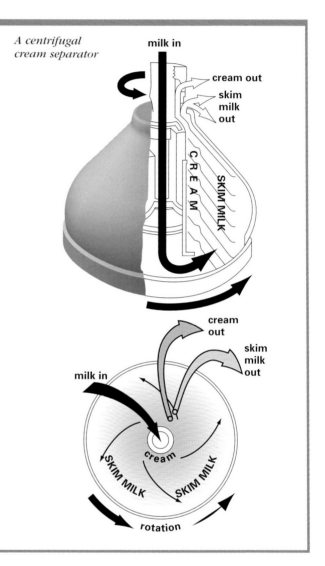

*A centrifugal cream separator*

## Structure

▶ Cream is an **emulsion** of fat in water.
▶ It is made up of:
   ◆ milk fat
   ◆ protein
   ◆ milk sugar (**lactose**)
   ◆ minerals
   ◆ vitamins (particularly vitamin A).

▶ There are different types of cream. Each type has a different amount of fat. The legal minimum fat content of some creams is shown below:
   ◆ double cream                48%
   ◆ whipping cream              35%
   ◆ single cream                18%
   ◆ clotted cream               63%
   ◆ sterilized cream (canned)   23%

# Quality

There are strict legal regulations controlling:
- how cream can be described
- what the cream is made of.

The Cream Regulations 1970 cover the milk fat contained in each cream.
- The label must describe the type of cream e.g. clotted, double etc.

The cream must contain the appropriate amount of milk fat (some of these amounts are shown at the bottom of page 26 and below).

The words used on the label may also tell the consumer how the cream can be used (i.e. the characteristics of the cream). For example:

| Fresh or frozen cream | Characteristics |
|---|---|
| Single cream | (18% fat) for pouring; will not whip |
| Whipping cream | (35% fat) for pouring; will whip to three times its original volume (amount) |
| Double cream | (48% fat) for pouring; will whip to twice its original volume; can be piped and used as a filling/topping etc. |
| Clotted cream | (63% fat) is thick and has a lumpy ('granular') texture; can be spread (e.g. scones and cream) |
| 'Coffee cream'/ half cream | (12% fat) pouring cream; can be used instead of single cream |
| Sour cream (single cream with a bacterial culture added to produce a thick texture and a sharp taste) | (18% fat) slight 'acid' taste, sometimes called 'crème fraîche'; good for savoury dishes |

| Fresh or frozen cream | Characteristics |
|---|---|
| Whipped cream | (35% fat) usually sold frozen; good for sweet dishes needing whipped cream, e.g. mousses, etc. |
| Extra thick textured cream | (30% fat) spoonable; will not whip. |
| Extra thick double cream | (48% fat) spoonable; will not whip. |
| Aerosol cream | (35% fat) for topping and piping; must be used soon after it has been squeezed out of the can because the foam collapses after 20–30 minutes |
| Sterilized cream | (23% fat) spoonable; will not whip; has a 'cooked' taste |
| Sterilized 'half cream | (12% fat) thin, for pouring; (taste as above) |

Cream is perishable and spoils quickly. Most cream on sale in the UK is pasteurized which lengthens storage time. Some is sterilized or ultra heat treated (UHT) (see page 61) which makes it keep longer, if not opened.

### Critical Points

◗ Cream will keep for about ten days in the coldest part of the refrigerator.

◗ It must be kept out of bright light which can make the cream **rancid**.

◗ Sterilized cream in an unopened can will keep for up to two years.

◗ UHT cream will keep for two to four months and does not need to be refrigerated until opened. After it is opened it must be treated as fresh cream.

◗ Cream absorbs smells and flavours from other foods, so it must not be stored near strong smelling, highly flavoured foods.

◗ Fresh cream cartons are stamped with two dates. One is the 'display until' date; the cream must be removed by the retailer if it hasn't sold by then. The other is the 'use by' date which shows the consumer when it must be eaten by.

## Nutritional value

**The nutritional value of 100 g of single cream and 100 g of double cream**

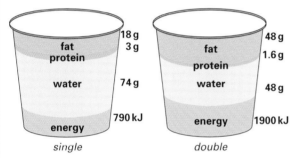

single

double

◗ The energy value varies because of the fat content. Single cream has less than half the energy value of double cream. Look back at the percentages of fat in each (page 26) to find the reason for this.

◗ 100 g double cream is roughly two-thirds of a small carton. People do not usually eat as much as that, so what is the nutritional value of the average amount that people

eat? The table below shows the nutritional value of 1 tablespoon of double cream (about 15g) and that of a heaped tablespoon of whipped cream (about 30 g)

|  | 1 tablespoon double cream (15 g) | 1 heaped tablespoon whipped cream (30 g) |  |
|---|---|---|---|
| Energy | 277 kJ | 555 kJ | Kilojoules |
| Protein | 0.3 g | 0.5 g | |
| Carbohydrate | 0.4 g | 0.8 g | |
| Fat | 7.2 g | 14.4 g | |
| Fibre | 0 g | 0 g | Grams |
| Vitamin C | 0.2 mg | 0.3 mg | |
| Calcium | 7.5 mg | 15 mg | |
| Iron | Trace | 0.1 mg | Milligrams |

## Functional properties

◗ **Homogenization** (where the globules of fat in the cream are made very small and are evenly distributed throughout the cream) improves the functional characteristics of cream. This is because it stops the fat globules 'clumping' together. The degree to which the cream is homogenized alters the

functional characteristics. For example:

◆ Single cream and half cream are often totally homogenized.

◆ Double cream may be lightly homogenized, particularly during warm weather to make sure it stays thick (i.e. keeps its viscosity).

◆ Extra thick textured cream and extra thick

double cream are heavily homogenized to make them thicker. These creams will not whip because the homogenization reduces the size of the fat globules so that they cannot 'clump' together, therefore the cream will not get any thicker.

▸ Cream for whipping must have a fat content of 35–42%. Fat content of around 35% achieves the best results.

▸ Most types of cream 'behave' well when heated. Cream has a low protein content so when it is heated there is not much coagulation. There are two advantages to this:

1 When cream is combined with an acid, e.g. tomato in cream of tomato soup, the mixture is less likely to curdle.

2 A skin does not form when cream is heated, e.g. when making a sauce.

## Foaming

▸ When cream is whipped, it changes from a liquid to a foam. This is how:

◆ Air is beaten into the cream, which makes bubbles in the cream.

◆ The protein in the cream changes its shape (i.e. it 'denatures') and surrounds the air bubbles. This protects the bubbles so that they do not burst and lose the air (they become **stabilized**).

◆ the fat globules stick to the protected bubbles. The high fat content of the cream makes it thicker and this keeps the bubbles evenly spaced in the cream (because it is too thick for them to rise to the surface).

▸ Successful foams are made:

◆ when the cream is cool, below 8°C. The fat globules become more solid the cooler the cream is and so a more successful foam is produced. Above 21°C little foam is produced

◆ when there is just sufficient beating. Underbeating won't add enough air. Overbeating makes the foam collapse and the fat globules 'clump' together.

▸ The type of cream used affects foaming:

◆ Cream with a high fat content (e.g. double cream) produces a stiff foam (about double its original volume).

◆ Whipping cream produces the largest amount of foam (about 3–4 times its original volume).

◆ Cream from Channel Island milk tends to 'foam' very quickly. It begins to form 'butter' if only slightly overbeaten.

## Combining cream with other ingredients

▸ Cream gives a 'rich' flavour to such products as soufflés and mousses.

▸ It produces a smooth texture when added to sauces, stews, etc.

▸ It can be successfully combined with many different ingredients, e.g. fruit, cereals, soups.

▸ Clotted cream can be spread straight from the carton which makes it an ideal combination with scones and jam. Its 'rich' colour, granular texture and 'crusty' appearance combine well with fruit, etc.

## Fact file

### Ice cream

Ice cream is a spin-off of milk production. Dairy ice cream contains milk and cream and has sugar, emulsifiers, stabilizers and flavourings added to it. Ice cream regulations determine whether ice cream can be described as dairy ice cream. They require dairy ice cream to contain not less than 7.5 per cent milk-solids-not-fat (called SNF in the industry) and not less than 5 per cent milk fat. Non-dairy ice cream is mostly made from skimmed milk and vegetable fat.

There are hard and soft types of ice cream. Hard ice cream contains more fat (often twice as much as soft ice cream).

## Structure

**Hens' eggs are: 10% shell**
**60% white**
**30% yolk**

The air space is formed as the eggs cools, after laying. As the egg gets older more air is sucked in. The air collects in a pocket called an air space. The bigger the air space, the older the egg.

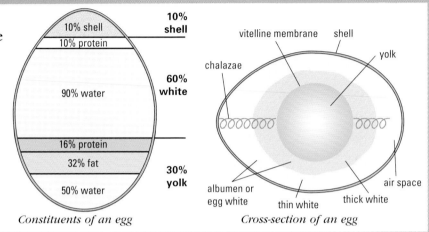

*Constituents of an egg*  *Cross-section of an egg*

## Quality

**Changes take place within an egg during storage.**

▶ The air space gets bigger (see above).

▶ Water moves into the yolk from the white. The yolk increases in size and becomes less viscous (jelly-like). The skin surrounding the yolk (the vitelline membrane) becomes weaker which means that the yolk could break into the white. This is a disadvantage in some cooking processes, for example, when it is necessary to separate the yolk and the egg white.

▶ The egg white becomes thinner because the amount of egg white protein decreases. This makes it easier to whisk egg white into a good foam.

▶ The pH rises (because carbon dioxide is lost from the egg). This can affect some cooking processes. For example, when the pH has risen, the egg becomes less acid and more alkaline which can lengthen the time it takes to make a good foam. (A pinch of cream of tartar speeds up foaming of an egg with a high pH.)

## Health and safety

In 1988 there was widespread concern about the presence of salmonella in eggs. This has now been brought under control and provided the following procedures are followed there is no danger in eating eggs.

▶ Eggs should be bought from a reputable supplier with a rapid turnover.

▶ Date marks must be checked to ensure 'fresh' eggs are bought. Micro-organisms can be drawn through the shell which increases the risk of contamination the longer the eggs are stored.

▶ Eggs are best stored on the lower shelves of fridges at home, or in shops in cool areas away from any source of warmth.

▶ Eggs absorb flavours so must be stored away from strongly flavoured foods.

## Nutritional value

**The nutritional value of egg (per 100g)**

| | | |
|---|---|---|
| Energy | 612 kJ | Kilojoules |
| Protein | 12.5 g | |
| Carbohydrate | 0 g | |
| Fat | 10.8 g | |
| Fibre | 0 g | Grams |
| Vitamin C | 0 mg | |
| Calcium | 57 mg | |
| Iron | 1.9 mg | Milligrams |

## Functional properties

### Eggs have properties that:

- thicken liquids and make them into solids (*coagulation*)
- help combinations of some ingredients to mix successfully (*emulsification*)
- lighten mixtures and produce 'open' textures (*foaming*)
- help combinations of ingredients to bind together and stay in the desired shape (*coagulation*)
- create a coating which protects a product from heat (*coagulation*).

## Coagulation

### Critical points

When eggs are heated the proteins in both the white and yolk 'stiffen'. This is called coagulation. If egg proteins are heated at too high a temperature or for too long coagulation produces a 'hard' and 'tough' mass which squeezes out any liquid present. Examples of this are 'rubbery' scrambled eggs and egg custards which have solid bits floating in a watery liquid.

When coagulation occurs the egg proteins have changed their appearance and texture. When this happens the proteins are said to be denatured.

### Points to remember

- At about 63°C thin egg white begins to coagulate.
- At about 66°C all egg white changes from having a 'flowing' consistency into having a firmer one.
- Egg yolk begins to set (thicken) at about 65°C and becomes solid at about 70°C.

## Emulsification

### Critical points

This property of eggs can be used to prevent mixtures of oil and other liquids separating. Egg yolk contains a substance called **lecithin** which acts as an **emulsifier**. When egg yolk is added to a mixture of oil and another liquid it is the lecithin in the yolk which prevents them from separating. An example is mayonnaise which is an emulsion of oil and vinegar stabilized by egg yolk.

### Points to remember

- Temperature is important. To emulsify and stabilize successfully, yolks should be at room temperature.
- The ingredients which are to be combined must be added to the yolk and not the other way round.

# Foaming

## Critical points

Egg white can increase in volume by as much as eight times when it is beaten. This happens because egg white traps air when beaten, and produces a large mass of bubbles called a foam. Scientifically speaking foam is a dispersion of gas (i.e. the air) within a liquid (i.e. the egg white).

The egg white protein (called albumen) forms a protective coating or network around the bubbles, which stops the liquid and air mixing. This stabilizes the foam, but if it is left to stand it will collapse. When the foam is heated the air cells in the foam grow bigger. The egg white protein coagulates to make a solid network of bubbles, and the foam changes from a liquid into a solid and is made permanent, as when baking a meringue.

Whole egg can also be beaten to form a foam but the volume will be less. This is because whole egg won't trap air as easily or in the same quantity as egg white alone. This type of foam is used in cake-making, for example it gives whisked sponge mixtures a light open texture.

## Points to remember

▶ If the white is not beaten enough the foam will be coarse, low in volume and watery. Insufficient coagulation takes place, so the bubbles burst and the foam collapses.

▶ If the white is beaten too much the foam is dull white in appearance. Over-coagulation takes place and the egg white membrane, which is stretched to hold the air bubbles and produce the foam, becomes too thin and breaks and the foam collapses.

▶ Egg white at room temperature (about 21°C) produces a stable foam more easily and quickly than a chilled egg white. However, if the white is too warm (30°C and above) a large volume can be produced but it will not be very stable.

▶ Eggs stored for a few days produce a more stable and larger foam than newly-laid eggs.

▶ Beating should stop when the foam is stiff enough to stand up in well defined peaks.

▶ Fat reduces the volume of the foam, so there should be no egg yolk in white which is used to make the foam.

▶ Salt reduces the stability of the foam.

▶ Adding sugar increases the time it takes to produce the foam because it slows down the denaturation of the egg white proteins. It is best to beat the egg whites to soft peaks before adding any sugar.

▶ The egg yolk is less likely to break if the egg is stored pointed end down.

| Stage | | Characteristics (description) | Uses |
|---|---|---|---|
| 1 | Slightly beaten | frothy, slightly foamy, large air bubbles | coating, thickening, emulsifying |
| 2 | Wet peak | stiff foam, air cells smaller/whiter, moves when bowl tipped, shiny/moist appearance, separates out if left to stand, makes rounded peaks when beaters lifted | soft meringues, mousses, sponge cakes |
| 3 | Stiff | air cells very small and white | hard meringue, soufflés |
| 4 | Over-beaten | dull white in appearance, flakes/lumps separate out, liquid gradually leaks out | products tend to be less successful |

# Combining eggs with other ingredients

**Binding**. Combinations of ingredients can be held together by the addition of whole raw egg. The egg proteins coagulate when heated and bind the ingredients to produce an unbroken, perfect result – as in fishcakes, rissoles etc.

**Thickening**. Liquids such as flavoured milk will thicken when mixed with eggs and heated. Examples include egg sauces and egg custards.

**Glazing**. A shiny brown finish on the surface of a product can be achieved if beaten egg is brushed on before cooking. The egg coagulates in the heat and makes a permanent glaze.

**Coating**. Beaten egg brushed on the surface of a product enables the cook to coat a product with, for example, breadcrumbs. The crumbs stick to the egg and are kept in place as the egg coagulates during cooking. The coating formed in this way acts as a protective layer between the product and heat source, thus preventing the product from becoming dry and overcooked.

**Emulsifying**. Egg yolk combined with a mixture of oil and another liquid produces a thick result which is stable. For example, in mayonnaise the egg yolk prevents the oil from separating from the vinegar.

## Fact file

### Free range eggs
Free range eggs come from hens that are allowed to wander in open air runs or large hen houses. These eggs are labelled 'free range' on the packaging and are different from 'farm fresh' eggs that often come from battery farms.

# 7 FISH

## What is fish?

### Sea fish

▶ **Dermersal** fish live at the bottom of the sea and include cod, haddock, plaice, sole, whiting and bream.

▶ **Pelagic** fish swim near the surface of the sea and include mackerel, herring and pilchards.

### Shellfish

▶ **Crustaceans** have legs and a shell that is jointed; they include crabs, prawns and shrimp.

▶ **Molluscs** have a hard outer shell and no legs. They are either bivalves, which have a hinged shell, such as mussels and scallops, or they have a snail-like shell, such as cockles.

### Freshwater fish

▶ Examples include trout, carp, pike and salmon.

### Oily and white fish

Sea fish and freshwater fish can be further sub-divided into oily fish and white fish.

▶ **Oily fish** contain between 10–20% fat in their flesh. Mackerel, herring and salmon are examples.

▶ **White fish** have less than 5% of fat in their flesh. Their fat/oil is in their liver. Haddock, cod and sole are examples.

*Just a few of the many different types of fish*

## Structure

Fish is made up of:
- ◆ water
- ◆ protein
- ◆ fat
- ◆ minerals.

▶ The average white fish is:

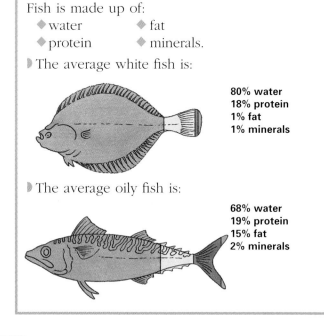

80% water
18% protein
1% fat
1% minerals

▶ The average oily fish is:

68% water
19% protein
15% fat
2% minerals

▶ The average edible part of shellfish (i.e. the part that is eaten) is:

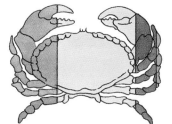

9% water
15% protein
4% fat
1% minerals

▶ The flesh of white fish and oily fish is made up of muscle and connective tissue.
- ◆ Fish muscle is arranged in segments (small pieces) of short fibres.
- ◆ The muscles are separated from each other by sheets of very thin connective tissue.
- ◆ Only about 3% of a fish's weight is connective tissue.

## Quality

▶Fresh fish has:
- ◆moist, firm flesh
- ◆bright red gills and bright clear eyes (if sold with the head on, e.g. herrings)
- ◆bright shiny scales which are very firmly attached to the skin
- ◆a fresh smell.

▶Smoked and salted f
herrings) and smoke
- ◆firm flesh and a sh
- ◆a 'good' smoky sm

▶All shellfish must:
- ◆have tightly closed shells (or they mus close tightly when tapped)
- ◆smell fresh (with no hint of an ammonia smell).

▶Lobsters, crabs and prawns must have shells that are bright and hard.

## Health and safety

Fish of all types spoil
become unsafe to eat. However, if the following points are noted there should be little danger.

▶Ideally fresh fish should be eaten on the day it is bought.

▶Fresh fish should be frozen or chilled straight away if it is not to be cooked on the day it is bought.

▶If fish is to be stored it should first be washed in cold water, dried and loosely wrapped in foil or clingfilm. It should be stored in the coolest part of the refrigerator and should not be stored for longer than

temperature is between 0°C and 5°C.)

▶Frozen fish must be stored at −18°C or below.

▶The temperature at which fish is cooked and the time allowed for cooking must be controlled by carefully following the instructions on the packet or in a recipe, so that any bacteria present in the fish are destroyed.

▶Shellfish must be chosen with great care and must be very fresh because they are common carriers of food poisoning organisms and can therefore be dangerous.

- All fish is rich in good quality protein.
- **Essential fatty acids** (such as linoleic acid) are part of the fat content of fish.
- The fatty acids in fish are unsaturated (see page 22).
- Oily fish are rich sources of the fat-soluble vitamins, A and D. Herring, in particular, is a rich source of vitamin D.
- Canned fish is a rich source of **calcium** if the bones are eaten along with the flesh. The bones are softened by the canning process. Canned sardines and pilchards are good examples.

## White fish

**The nutritional value of 100 g of raw cod fillet and 100 g of cod that has been dipped in batter and fried**

### 100 g of raw cod fillet

| | | |
|---|---|---|
| Energy | 80 kcal 337 kJ | Kilocalories Kilojoules |
| Protein | 18.3 g | |
| Fat | 0.7 g | |
| Carbohydrate | 0 g | |
| Water | 80.8 g | Grams |
| Calcium | 9 mg | |
| Iron | 0.1 mg | |
| Thiamin | 0.04 mg | |
| Riboflavin | 0.05 mg | |
| Nicotinic acid | 2.4 mg | Milligrams |
| Vitamin C | Trace | |
| Vitamin D | Trace | Micrograms |

### 100 g of cod fried in batter

| | | |
|---|---|---|
| Energy | 247 kcal 1031 kJ | Kilocalories Kilojoules |
| Protein | 16.1 g | |
| Fat | 15.4 g | |
| Carbohydrate | 11.7 g | |
| Water | 54.9 g | Grams |
| Calcium | 67 mg | |
| Iron | 0.5 mg | |
| Thiamin | 0.09 mg | |
| Riboflavin | 0.09 mg | |
| Nicotinic acid | 1.7 mg | Milligrams |
| Vitamin C | Trace | |
| Vitamin D | Trace | Micrograms |

## Oily fish

**The nutritional value of 100 g of grilled mackerel**

### 100 g grilled mackerel

| | | |
|---|---|---|
| Energy | 239 kcal 994 kJ | Kilocalories Kilojoules |
| Protein | 20.8 g | |
| Fat | 17.3 g | |
| Carbohydrate | 0 g | |
| Water | 58.6 g | Grams |
| Calcium | 12 mg | |
| Iron | 0.8 mg | |
| Thiamin | 0.15 mg | |
| Riboflavin | 0.32 mg | |
| Nicotinic acid | 9.4 mg | Milligrams |
| Vitamin C | Trace | |
| Vitamin D | 5.4 µg | Micrograms |

## Canned fish

**The nutritional value of 100 g of pilchards canned in tomato sauce**

### 100 g pilchards in tomato sauce

| | | |
|---|---|---|
| Energy | 144 kcal 601 kJ | Kilocalories Kilojoules |
| Protein | 16.7 g | |
| Fat | 8.1 g | |
| Carbohydrate | 1.1 g | |
| Water | 70.4 g | Grams |
| Calcium | 250 mg | |
| Iron | 2.5 mg | |
| Thiamin | 0.01 mg | |
| Riboflavin | 0.33 mg | |
| Nicotinic acid | 5.9 mg | Milligrams |
| Vitamin C | Trace | |
| Vitamin D | 14 µg | Micrograms |

*Notice that the calcium content of these pilchards is higher than that of the 100 g of grilled mackerel.*

- The cooking method used can have an effect on the nutritional value of fish. The chart of the nutritional value of 100 g of raw cod fillet and 100 g of cod fried in batter (left) shows that the fat content of the fried cod is much higher because the batter absorbs some of the cooking fat.

## Recipe

### Mackerel pâté

1 clove finely chopped garlic
50 g unsalted butter
250 g tinned mackerel in brine
1 level teaspoon horseradish cream
salt and pepper
1 tablespoon mayonnaise

Sauté the garlic in 25 g butter until soft.

Drain the mackerel.

Mash the mackerel with the horseradish cream, salt and pepper and mayonnaise.

Beat the garlic into the mixture.

Put the mixture into a dish. Smooth the top.

Melt the remaining butter and pour on top.

Refrigerate.

Serve with fingers of hot toast.

## Functional properties

- Fish flesh is made up of muscle and some connective tissue (see 'Structure', page 34).
  - The connective tissue is weak and dissolves easily.
  - The short muscle fibres and small amount of weak connective tissue make fish tender and delicate, which means it has a tendency to break on cooking.

### The main characteristics arise as a result of:

- the small amount and type of connective tissue present
- the delicate structure of the muscle fibres
- the amount of oil present in the flesh.

## The effect of cooking on fish

### Critical points

- During cooking, the fish muscle segments shrink and moisture is squeezed out. This is why moderate temperatures and quick methods of cooking are used. If fish is cooked at a high temperature for longer than the time necessary to make the fish safe and attractive to eat, the result is often tough, dry and flavourless – because the segments have shrunk so much that all the moisture is squeezed out. However, the fish must be cooked long enough to make it safe to eat. It is important to follow instructions about cooking time carefully (see 'Health and safety', page 35).

- The fish muscle segments may separate and break into pieces if cooked at too high a temperature. This occurs because the connective tissue weakens and dissolves. This happens very easily with haddock.

- The connective tissue is made of **collagen**. It dissolves easily when it is heated and changes into **gelatin**.

- In oily fish, the fat content helps to keep the flesh moist and prevents it from drying out.

- Some of the B vitamins are lost since they are destroyed by heat. However, most fish is not a rich source of these vitamins so the loss is not so important.

- Any liquid left behind after cooking fish can be used in a sauce to serve with the fish. This will replace any moisture squeezed out of the fish during cooking and can help to

*Fish cooked and served in three different ways*

# The effects of chilling and freezing on fish

## Critical points

▶ Fish must be chilled or frozen soon after it is caught because the enzymes which cause fish to spoil can work at low temperatures. Also, fish oils oxidize (take in oxygen) at fairly low temperatures and this can give the fish a 'rancid' flavour.

▶ Ice is the best medium for chilling fish because it absorbs any latent (hidden) heat from the fish and as the ice melts the fish is chilled. This extends the shelf-life of fish for several days. Fishermen pack fish in ice on their boats as soon as it is caught. This makes sure that when it reaches the quay, to be sold or transported to a fish market, it is as fresh as possible.

▶ Freezing allows fish to be stored for several months. The fish is best frozen quickly at a temperature of about −30°C. Large fishing fleets have quick-freezing facilities on board the ships and the fish are frozen immediately after the 'catch' is landed and prepared (i.e. gutted, etc.).

*Fish is usually packed in ice from the time it is caught to the time it is sold in the fishmonger's shop*

## Disadvantages of freezing fish

▶ Ice crystals form in the flesh of the fish. If the freezing process takes a long time the crystals are large and damage the fibres in the flesh. Large crystals also result in more water being lost when the fish thaws (this is called 'drip').

▶ Protein changes when moisture is lost from the fish. On thawing, the fish may be tough and stringy and produce a disappointing texture when cooked.

▶ The flesh can dry out. This happens because moisture from the surface of the fish moves to the surroundings – for example, to air pockets in the wrapping or the carton in which the fish is kept or to any air present between layers of fish. This drying out is known as 'freezer burn'. It occurs because the ice has changed into a gas without first becoming liquid.

# Combining fish with other ingredients

▶ Certain types of raw fish can be mixed with vinegar, which extends the shelf-life of the fish and makes it safe and appetizing to eat. This is because bacteria cannot live in an acid environment (a low pH). The vinegar, or other acid, extends the shelf-life by lowering the pH of the mixture. Pickled herrings and roll mops are preserved in this way. Other examples of where acid is used to make fish safe and appetizing to eat are special marinade mixtures that also give the fish a particular flavour, such as the following sweet sour mixture:

150 ml sesame oil
55 ml white wine vinegar
juice of 2 limes
1 teaspoon 'hot' sauce such as Tabasco or hot chilli sauce
1 level teaspoon white sugar
1 tablespoon Worcestershire sauce
salt and pepper

This mixture is poured over the fish, e.g. about 250 g raw herring, and left for 48 hours. The vinegar and lime juice are the acid ingredients.

Fish is combined with salt to preserve it.

Fish is combined with other ingredients such as breadcrumbs, sauces, potatoes, etc. to produce a variety of products. Fish fingers are made from blocks of frozen fish sawn into fingers which are then covered 'enrobed' in an egg and breadcrumb coating. This relatively simple idea started in the 1950s and is now a multi-million pound industry. Other examples are fish pies topped with potato, pastry, cheese and tomato, etc. All these combinations produce a variety of textures and tastes.

Dishes for a particular purpose can be made from fish combined with other ingredients. One example is fishcakes, where mixing a small amount of fish with potatoes, which are a cheaper ingredient, can make an economical product. In industry this is called extending or bulking the product. Other examples include products that may be described as low in fat (e.g. white fish, lemon and cucumber bake) or as high in fibre (e.g. fish, banana and brown crumb crumble). The nutritional value of a dish can be improved by combining white fish with other ingredients (e.g. with milk in a sauce, with cheese, with egg, or with rice and spices as in kedgeree).

*To coat fishfingers evenly with batter, they pass through an enrobing machine*

*Fishcakes combine fish and potato to make an economical product*

## Recipe

### Fishcakes

4 plain cutters (5 cm)
1 teaspoon cooking oil
110 g potatoes (boiled with skins on)
salt and pepper
1 heaped dessert spoon chopped parsley
1 small onion chopped very finely
110 g cooked fish (e.g. cod)
25 g butter
1 tablespoon cooking oil

Heat oven to 200°C 400°F, gas mark 6

Grease the inside of the cutters with the teaspoon of cooking oil.
Peel the cooked potatoes. Cut into slices.
Put a layer of potato slices in the bottom of each cutter. Add salt and pepper.
Put a layer of parsley, onion and fish on top. Press down.
Cover with a layer of potato. Press down.
Heat the oil and butter in a frying pan.
Using a palette knife put each cake (in the cutter) into the frying pan. Fry gently on both sides until golden brown and crisp.
Put the cakes (still in cutters) onto a baking tray. Gently remove the cutters.
Cook in the oven for 10 minutes.

## What is fruit?

A fruit is the ripe ovary of a flower. There are different types of fruit which vary according to the kinds of flower from which they develop. For example, pears and apples develop from a simple flower. Strawberries develop from a more complicated flower.

*Strawberries develop from a complex flower*

**There are four main groups of fruit:**

◆ **fruit with stones**, such as plums, cherries, damsons, greengages, apricots, nectarines and peaches
◆ **soft** or **berry fruit**, such as strawberries, raspberries, loganberries, grapes, blackberries, blackcurrants and redcurrants

◆ **hard fruit**, such as apples and pears
◆ **citrus fruit**, such as oranges, lemons, limes, mandarins, clementines, tangerines, satsumas, grapefruit, kumquat, pomelo, ugli and tangelo.

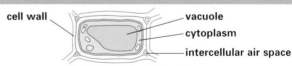

citrus fruit     fruit with stones

soft or berry fruit     hard fruit

*The four main groups of fruit*

**Fruits that do not fall into those groups include:**

◆ rhubarb, quince and the so-called tropical fruits, banana, pineapple, figs, persimmon, pomegranate, prickly pear, passion fruit, melons of different kinds, kiwi fruit, pawpaw, guava and mango.

## Structure

▶ The edible part of fruits is made up of cells that have:
◆ an outer wall (mostly **cellulose**)
◆ a jelly-like substance inside (called **cytoplasm**)
◆ cell sap (a watery solution of sugars, vitamins, pigments and mineral salts)
◆ air spaces between the cells (known as intercellular air spaces).
▶ The largest part of the cell contains the cell sap, it is called the **vacuole**.

cell wall     vacuole
cytoplasm
intercellular air space

*A cross-section through a plant cell*

▶ Fruit contains a lot of moisture.

▶ Cellulose thickens the cell walls of fruit; the older the plant, the thicker the walls.

▶ Between the cell walls there is a tough, insoluble material called **protopectin**. This becomes softer and soluble as the fruit ripens. This soluble form is called **pectin**.

# Quality

## Fresh fruit

All fruit needs to ripen before it is eaten. Ripening is the sudden and big change in the life of fruit. This is what happens:

- The fruit grows to full size.
- The production of **ethylene** (a simple hydrocarbon gas) within the fruit starts the ripening process.
- The colour changes. The chlorophyll (i.e. the green colour) is destroyed and other colour pigments are free to develop in the fruit.
- The **starch** changes to **sugar**. This varies according to the type of fruit (e.g. melons, citrus fruit and pineapples do not store starch; their supply comes from the leaves of the plant, therefore their final sugar content stays the same as it was when the fruit was picked).
- The edible part (e.g. the 'flesh' of the fruit) becomes tender. This happens because some **enzymes** in fruit (the pectinesterases) make the cell walls more soluble and eventually they dissolve. This makes the fruit softer and juicier. If the cell walls dissolve completely the fruit becomes 'mushy'.
- A 'fruity' odour develops and the quantity of acid is reduced.

The ripening process is what makes fruit attractive to eat, but all fruit will continue to ripen until it spoils.

*Strawberries ripening*

Commercially grown fruit is often under-ripe when picked. The fruit is ripened before sale in special storage places where the temperature and humidity of the air are controlled. This allows fruit to be transported all over the world.

All fruit should be ripe, fresh and have a good colour when eaten. Under-ripe fruit does not have full flavour. Bruised and wrinkled fruit will be past its best quality (except for passion fruit, where the skin of a ripe fruit must be wrinkly).

Fruit should feel firm and heavy for its size.

Citrus fruits such as oranges, lemons and limes should feel 'plump' but not puffy or spongy. Spongy fruit has thick skin and little juice.

Fruit will be at its cheapest when it is in season. Price is not always an indication of quality. The cost of fruit varies in relation to:

- how much is available (i.e. supply)
- what the consumer wants (i.e. demand).

See the chart of seasons for fruit below.

## Seasons for British fruit

| Fruit | Jan. | Feb. | Mar. | Apr. | May | Jun. | Jul. | Aug. | Sep. | Oct. | Nov. | Dec. |
|---|---|---|---|---|---|---|---|---|---|---|---|---|
| Apples (eating) | ✔ | ✔ | ✔ | ✔ | | | ✔ | ✔ | ✔ | ✔ | ✔ | ✔ |
| Apples (cooking) | ✔ | ✔ | ✔ | ✔ | ✔ | ✔ | ✔ | ✔ | ✔ | ✔ | ✔ | ✔ |
| Blackberries | | | | | | ✔ | ✔ | ✔ | ✔ | ✔ | | |
| Blackcurrants | | | | | | | ✔ | ✔ | | | | |
| Cherries | | | | | | ✔ | ✔ | ✔ | | | | |
| Gooseberries | | | | | | ✔ | ✔ | | | | | |
| Grapes | | | | | | | | | ✔ | ✔ | ✔ | ✔ |
| Peaches | | | | | | ✔ | ✔ | ✔ | | | | |
| Pears | ✔ | ✔ | ✔ | | | | | ✔ | ✔ | ✔ | ✔ | ✔ |
| Plums | | | | | | | | ✔ | ✔ | ✔ | | |
| Raspberries | | | | | | ✔ | ✔ | ✔ | ✔ | | | |
| Redcurrants | | | | | | | ✔ | ✔ | | | | |
| Rhubarb | ✔ | ✔ | ✔ | ✔ | ✔ | ✔ | | | | | | ✔ |
| Strawberries | | | | | | ✔ | ✔ | ✔ | | | | |

## Preserving fruit

Some fruits are dried, canned, frozen, mixed with sugar and/or vinegar to lengthen their shelf-life (i.e. to preserve them).

▶ Examples of dried fruit include prunes, figs, raisins, currants, sultanas and dried apricots. Currants, raisins and sultanas, etc. are usually sold washed and are ready for use. Dried apricots, prunes and figs, etc. may need to be soaked (i.e. hydrated)

▶ Canned fruits include pineapple, peaches, mandarins, plums, rhubarb, etc. They are usually in a liquid such as sugar syrup.

▶ Most fruit can be frozen. Freezing is especially useful for soft and berried fruit, particularly raspberries. However, strawberries become very watery and 'mushy' on thawing. This is because the crystals of ice damage the cell walls, so that when the fruit thaws the cells can no longer hold the liquid. The liquid 'leaks' out of the fruit and the flesh of the fruit loses its crispness.

▶ Processing fruit with sugar and/or vinegar extends shelf-life as in jam, marmalade, pickles etc. The sugar increases the sugar content and reduces/prevents the growth of micro-organisms. Vinegar increases the acidity which also prevents or reduces the growth of micro-organisms. If, however, there is any evaporation of moisture on the surface of the product, moulds and yeasts may grow and cause spoilage.

## Health and safety

▶ Fresh fruit should be used very quickly after it is picked or bought. This is because all fruit continues to ripen after it has been picked. During the ripening process fruit takes in oxygen, gives off carbon dioxide and warms up.

▶ Fruits are acidic and usually have a high sugar content which keeps them protected against microbial spoilage to some extent. However, the high sugar content makes some types of fruit become mouldy very quickly. Soft and berried fruits are examples.

▶ Most fruit should be kept in a cool, dark place until used. Berried fruits are best kept in the refrigerator. Bananas spoil faster if they are too chilled so normal room temperature is best for them.

▶ All dried fruit should be free of moisture to preserve its quality during storage.

▶ Canned fruit with dents or bubbles in the can should not be bought. The bubbles may mean that the can is 'blown' because the fruit inside is giving off a gas. This means the fruit is being spoilt as a result of bacterial activity. Cans usually have a 'best before' date printed on them.

*Cans usually have a 'best before' date printed on them*

# Nutritional value

Fruit is generally low in energy, high in **vitamin C** and provides dietary fibre, especially if the skin of the fruit is eaten.

## The nutritional value of 100 g of various fresh and preserved fruits

| | Apples | Bananas | Dates (dried) | Oranges | |
|---|---|---|---|---|---|
| Inedible wastage | 20% | 40% | 14% | 30% | Per cent |
| Energy | 46 kcal 197 kJ | 76 kcal 326 kJ | 248 kcal 1056 kJ | 35 kcal 150 kJ | Kilocalories Kilojoules |
| Protein | 0.3 g | 1.1 g | 2 g | 0.8 g | |
| Carbohydrate | 12 g | 19.2 g | 63.9 g | 8.5 g | |
| Water | 84 g | 71 g | 15 g | 86 g | Grams |
| Calcium | 4 mg | 7 mg | 68 mg | 41 mg | |
| Iron | 0.3 mg | 0.4 mg | 1.6 mg | 0.3 mg | |
| Vitamin C | 5 mg | 10 mg | 0 mg | 50 mg | |
| Thiamin | 0.04 mg | 0.04 mg | 0.07 mg | 0.1 mg | |
| Riboflavin | 0.02 mg | 0.07 mg | 0.04 mg | 0.03 mg | |
| Nicotinic acid equivalent | 0.1 mg | 0.8 mg | 2.3 mg | 0.3 mg | Milligrams |
| Vitamin A | 5 µg | 33 µg | 10 µg | 8 µg | Micrograms |

| | Pears (fresh) | Strawberries | Peaches (canned) | |
|---|---|---|---|---|
| Inedible wastage | 25% | 3% | 0% | Per cent |
| Energy | 41 kcal 175 kJ | 26 kcal 109 kJ | 88 kcal 373 kJ | Kilocalories Kilojoules |
| Protein | 0.3 g | 0.6 g | 0.4 g | |
| Carbohydrate | 10.6 g | 6.2 g | 22.9 g | |
| Water | 83 g | 89 g | 74 g | Grams |
| Calcium | 8 mg | 22 mg | 4 mg | |
| Iron | 0.2 mg | 0.7 mg | 1.9 mg | |
| Vitamin C | 3 mg | 60 mg | 4 mg | |
| Thiamin | 0.03 mg | 0.02 mg | 0.01 mg | |
| Riboflavin | 0.03 mg | 0.03 mg | 0.02 mg | |
| Nicotinic acid equivalent | 0.3 mg | 0.5 mg | 0.6 mg | Milligrams |
| Vitamin A | 2 µg | 5 µg | 41 µg | Micrograms |

Notice the difference in energy value between dried dates and fresh apples. The reason for that difference is that dried fruit is processed by removing all moisture from the fruit. This means that the sugar content becomes higher than that of the fresh fruit, so dried fruit has a higher energy value.

A direct comparison of energy value is:

| 100 g dried raw apricots | 182 kcal / 776 kJ energy |
|---|---|
| 100 g fresh raw apricots | 28 kcal / 117 kJ energy |

Canned fruit usually has less vitamin C than fresh fruit because the heat used during the canning process destroys some of this vitamin. If the fruit is canned in syrup and both fruit and juice are eaten the energy value is increased.

Most fruits are best eaten raw, provided they are ripe.

## Cell walls

▶When fruits are cut, chopped or shredded, etc. the cell walls are broken. This allows an enzyme in the cells to mix with and destroy the vitamin C. The enzyme is called **ascorbic acid oxydase**. It is destroyed by heat. To cut down the loss of vitamin C:

◆keep fruit as whole as possible. If it has to be cut a sharp knife should be used and the fruit should not be cut, chopped or shredded more than is necessary. Large pieces are best

◆if the fruit is to be cooked put it into a boiling cooking medium for as short a time as possible. This will destroy the enzyme and save more of the vitamin C.

Vitamin C leaks into water (i.e. it is water soluble), so:

◆fruit should not be soaked in water

◆any juice or syrup that the fruit is cooked in should be served with it (the vitamin C will have dissolved in the liquid).

▶When the cell walls of fruit are heated they soften. The heat weakens the cell walls and water leaks out of them. This makes fruit tender. Water will continue to leak from the cells if cooking continues. This will overcook the fruit and it will become 'mushy'. The effects of heat on fruit are similar to those on vegetables (see page 87).

▶If sugar is needed, it should be added at the end of the cooking time. Sugar can toughen the cells of the fruit if added at the beginning, before the heat has had time to soften them.

## Browning

▶When some fresh fruit is cut or peeled the outside surfaces darken and eventually turn brown. Apples, peaches, pears and bananas are examples. This is caused by enzymes in the fruit linking with oxygen in the air. It is called **enzymic browning**.

▶The browning is prevented:

**a** if the cut surfaces are sealed from the air, for example by putting an acid or sugary solution such as lemon juice or a sugar syrup on the cut surface

**b** if the fruit is kept cool, because this slows down the action of the enzymes and delays browning

**c** if the fruit is prepared just before use

**d** if the fruit is 'blanched' (put in boiling water for a few seconds and then cooled quickly). This changes the enzymes (i.e. denatures them) so that they do not link with oxygen.

▶Fruits contain enzymes and organic substances called **phenols**. The enzymes and phenols are separated from each other in whole fruit, but when the fruit is cut or damaged they join together. When the enzymes and phenols join they take oxygen from the air and enzymic browning occurs. If cut fruit is mixed with an acid, such as ascorbic acid (vitamin C), the acid takes all the available oxygen from the air and enzymic browning is prevented. In this case the acid is known as a **reducing agent**.

*There are various ways of preventing browning, such as adding a sugar syrup to the cut surface*

# Combining fruit with other ingredients

There are nutritional, textural, functional and taste effects of combining fruit with other ingredients.

**Nutritional effects**. Fruit is a rich source of vitamin C and dietary fibre. So when, for example, an orange salad is served with a meat or fish dish, it increases the vitamin C provision in a meal. When blackcurrants, raspberries and redcurrants are combined with, for example, pastry, crumble mixtures, ice creams, etc., they provide extra dietary fibre.

**Textural effects**. Most fruit is moist and has a 'bite'. It provides crispness and/or moisture when combined with dishes such as custards or salads (e.g. Waldorf salad, where slices of crisp eating apple are included).

**Functional effects**. Certain fruit contains substances that affect the texture and/or viscosity (thickness) and gelling properties of other ingredients. Examples include:

- the use of enzymes from fruit to help tenderize meat (e.g. bromelin, an enzyme in fresh pineapple). The enzyme begins to digest the muscle fibres and connective tissues
- the acid from fruits (e.g. lemons) can cause a mixture thickened by the gelatinization of starch to lose its thickness
- enzymes in certain fresh fruit break down the protein in other ingredients. These enzymes are called **proteolytic enzymes**. For example, if fresh pineapple is added to a jelly, it will not set. The proteolytic enzyme in pineapple (bromelin) will digest the protein and the jelly will remain liquid. If the pineapple is heated first (as in canned pineapple) the bromelin is destroyed and the jelly will set
- pectin from fruits such as plums and apples makes mixtures set or gel. Jam is an example of the use of pectin.

**Taste and aesthetic effects**. Different fruits improve the taste and appearance of many products. Examples include grated orange rind and/or flesh in mousse, soufflé, sauces, etc; pears in a chocolate mixture such as a sauce; bananas served with a spicy or curry sauce.

*Fruit used in combination with other ingredients*

# Fact file

## Five-a-day!

A diet that is low in fatty and sugary foods and high in fruit, vegetables and starchy foods is best for your health. It is recommended that people should eat five servings of fruit and vegetables a day.

Most people do not eat enough fruit and vegetables. Nutrition experts and doctors say that some people need to double the amount they eat. We should all eat about 400 g (1lb) of fruit and vegetables per day for a balanced diet.

Two different vegetables, in addition to potatoes, can be served with every main meal.

Combinations of vegetables of different textures, tastes and colours can be used in various methods of cooking (e.g. stir-fry).

Fruit should be included in snacks, packed lunches and on snack food counters in schools, sandwich bars, etc.

Canned, frozen and seasonal fresh fruits and vegetables should be used to provide variety.

# 9 HERBS

## What are herbs?

Herbs are naturally occurring food flavourings. Some herbs are also used to make medicines.

▶ Herbs are available whole, chopped or ground (i.e. powdered), either fresh, dried, frozen or freeze-dried.

▶ Pot grown fresh herbs are available throughout the year. These are grown in the UK, mostly in East Anglia, the Vale of Evesham and the West Midlands.

▶ Fresh herbs are imported throughout the year, especially in winter. They come from many countries including Cyprus, Portugal, Spain, Holland and France (mainly Brittany).

▶ Dried herbs are imported from countries such as Egypt, Turkey and Algeria.

▶ Recent mild winters have enabled UK growers to produce fresh herbs during the early winter months. The south of England is the main area for this.

▶ Fresh herbs generally give better results than dried ones.

▶ Dried herbs are stronger in flavour. This is because the water has been removed, making the flavour more concentrated. Care should be taken to control the amount used. A general guide to follow is one level teaspoon of dried herbs gives the flavouring effect of one heaped teaspoon of fresh herbs.

## Structure

▶ Herbs are soft stemmed, non-woody plants. The flower, leaves, seeds, stems or roots are used as flavourings, depending on the herb.

▶ The odour and taste of herbs comes from their **volatile oils**. They provide a variety of food flavours.

## Functional properties of various herbs

| Herb | Part used | Functional properties |
|---|---|---|
| **Angelica** This plant belongs to the same family as parsley. | Mainly the stem, which is preserved in sugar. However the whole plant can be used. | Small pieces of the candied stem are used as cake decoration. It is usually a very attractive green colour. |
| **Basil** Sweet basil is the best known. | The leaves. | It has a strong flavour, so small amounts only should be used; if too much is used a bitter flavour develops. Basil is a popular flavouring in Italian dishes and is good with tomato and most meat and cheese dishes. It is sometimes preserved in oil to lengthen its shelf-life. The oil can be used to flavour salad dressings, etc. |
| **Bay** | The leaves. It is available dried or ground. | It combines well with meats, milk, poultry, etc. It is mixed with other herbs to make a bouquet garni which is used to flavour meat, poultry and vegetable dishes. |

| Herb | Part used | Functional properties |
|------|-----------|----------------------|
| **Chives**<br>This belongs to the onion family. | The leaves. They are dark green hollow stems. They have a delicate flavour and can be chopped, snipped with scissors or left whole. | Chopped or snipped they make good additions to salads, rice and pasta dishes, etc. If left whole they provide a good garnish (e.g. whole pieces of chive arranged in a criss-cross pattern on top of grilled fish for an attractive effect). They lose some of their flavour when cooked. |
| **Coriander**<br>This is a member of the carrot family. | Both the seeds and the leaves are used. | The leaves are bright green and are chopped and added to or sprinkled over spicy food. Coriander is an important ingredient in curries, etc. The seeds are used whole or ground for both sweet and savoury dishes (e.g. whole seeds in casseroles and stews and ground seeds in cakes and puddings). Their flavour is lemony with a touch of sage. |
| **Dill** | The stalk, seeds and leaves. | The stalks and seeds particularly are used in many pickle recipes both domestically and commercially. The leaves are used with many fish dishes, such as marinated salmon. |
| **Horseradish** | The roots. | The root is grated and then used either for making horseradish sauce to serve with beef or for flavouring other dishes such as stews, soups and salad dressings. It combines well with cream, beetroot, cheese and fish such as mackerel and smoked fish of any kind. |
| **Lemon grass** | The stalks. | Citric oils in the grass give a lemon flavour. It combines well with fish and lightly spiced ingredients. |

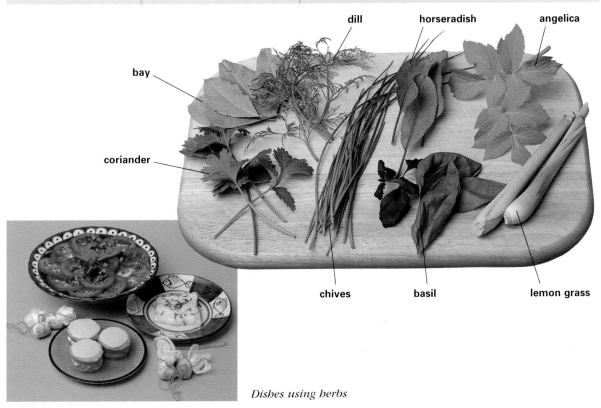

*Dishes using herbs*

| Herb | Part used | Functional properties |
|---|---|---|
| **Marjoram** | The leaves are used; they have a sweet, spicy flavour. | It can be used instead of oregano. Both of these herbs combine well with potatoes, eggs and tomatoes and are good in stews, particularly beef stews. |
| **Mint**<br>There are many types of mint. The most common is spearmint. Apple mint has a finer, more delicate flavour and large, white hairy leaves. | The leaves | The leaves combine well with vinegar or another acid to make mint sauce. They also make a very good jelly. Mint sauce and mint jelly combine well with meat, particularly lamb. If mint leaves are put in the water used to boil vegetables they add flavour, particularly to new potatoes and peas. |
| **Parsley**<br>There are a number of different types of parsley, including broad-leaved, curly-leafed and Hamburg. | The leaves and stalks. | The stalks can be tied in a bundle with celery, a strip of carrot and some lemon rind and used to flavour white meat and vegetable stews and soups (e.g. chicken fricassee, cauliflower soup, etc.). It is also used with other herbs to make a bouquet garni. The leaves are chopped to give the strongest flavour. They are used in stuffings, sauces, parsley-flavoured butter, etc. Small bunches of the leaves make a good garnish. Parsley combines well with many ingredients (e.g. rice, pasta, fish and egg). |
| **Rosemary** | The leaves. They are narrow, like small needles and hard in texture. | The taste and odour of rosemary comes from the oil the leaves contain. It is oil of camphor. Rosemary combines well with lamb and garlic dishes. |
| **Sage** | The leaves. | The flavour can be very strong so sage should be used in small amounts. It combines well with onion and bread in stuffings. It goes well with pork, bacon, poultry and cheese dishes. The flavour can overpower other ingredients with a more delicate flavour such as fish. |
| **Tarragon**<br>There are two varieties, French and Russian. Russian tarragon has a coarser leaf and is believed to give an inferior flavour to the French variety. | The stem and leaves. | Tarragon combines well with fish, poultry and eggs. However, the flavour is delicate and care should be taken that it is not overwhelmed by other stronger flavours in a dish. The leaves are used to flavour vinegar, which is then used to make salad dressings. It is an essential flavouring ingredient in egg sauces such as béarnaise and hollandaise. |
| **Thyme** | The stem and leaves. | A stem with leaves can be tied in a bundle with parsley, celery, strips of carrot and lemon rind to flavour strong meats such as beef and some cheese dishes. The leaves are very small and need little chopping. They are added to stuffings, often combined with parsley. Lemon thyme smells faintly of lemon but gives a flavour very similar to other varieties of thyme. |

marjoram  rosemary  sage  thyme

parsley  tarragon  mint

*Dishes using herbs*

## Fact file

Fresh herbs such as whole basil, chervil, coriander leaves as well as parsley and mint are available in most supermarkets. These help to give ordinary salad more flavour, and can be bought as ready-prepared mixtures of fresh herbs which are wonderful time savers.

Remember that dried herbs are twice as strong as fresh ones so, for example, if the recipe states one heaped teaspoon of a fresh herb, a level teaspoon of the dried herb will be sufficient.

## What is margarine?

- Most margarines are blends of refined oils and fats, skimmed milk cultures, whey, brine and other flavourings, vitamins A and D, colourings, emulsifiers and other permitted ingredients.
- The oils used include oil from 'oily' fish (e.g. herring), palm oil, and sunflower, soya and sesame oils.
- The oils are hardened by bubbling hydrogen gas through them. This process (called **hydrogenation**) alters the oil, turning it from a liquid into a solid.
- Flavour is produced by whey (left over after making cheese) or a special bacteria which acts on the lactose in the milk or milk-free liquid. Salt is also added for flavour.
- Vitamins A and D must, as a legal requirement, be added during manufacture.
- **Carotene** and **annatto** are added to colour the margarine.
- Emulsifying agents (to give a smooth consistency and texture) and anti-splattering agents (to prevent spitting during heating) are also added.

*Palm trees are cultivated for their oil*

## Structure

- Margarine was developed as a substitute for butter. Its structure is, therefore, similar to that of butter.
- It is an emulsion of edible fats/oils and skimmed milk or water.
- It is made up of:
  - ◆ fat
  - ◆ water
  - ◆ vitamins.
- The average composition is:
  - ◆ 81.5% fat
  - ◆ 15% water.

## Health and safety

- The same points apply as for butter (see page 5).
- The Margarine Regulations of 1967 state that margarine must be at least 80% fat and no more than 16% moisture.
- There should be:
  - ◆ 942–960 µg vitamin A per 100 g
  - ◆ 8–10 µg vitamin D per 100 g
- Low fat spreads must be used within two weeks of purchase because their low fat and high water content provide a medium for mould growth.

# Quality

Margarine can be made to different specifications to vary the hardness, texture, consistency, spreadability, creamability, etc. For example:

- premium, high-price types with added butter, for spreading on bread, toast, etc.
- block or hard margarine for cooking; particularly for pastry making, including flaky, croissant, and Danish pastry, because it can be rolled into layers between the dough layers (see page 24)
- soft types for easy creaming or one-stage ('all in one') methods used for cakes, sauces, etc.; or for spreading straight from the fridge
- margarines made from vegetable oils which contain less hydrogen. These are described as 'low in saturates'.

Low fat spreads are not called margarine because their composition does not meet the margarine regulations. The fat content is low and the water content is very high. Because of the high water content these spreads cannot be used for cooking, although some manufacturers supply recipes for them which are successful.

Kosher margarine such as Tomor, is made from vegetable oils. No fat from animals is used and its production is strictly supervised to meet Jewish dietary laws.

# Nutritional value

**The nutritional value of margarine (per 100 g)**

| | | |
|---|---|---|
| Energy | 735 kcal  3019 kJ | Kilocalories / Kilojoules |
| Protein | 0.2 g | |
| Fat | 81.5 g | |
| Water | 15 g | Grams |
| Vitamin A (retinol equivalent) | 942–960 µg | |
| Vitamin D | 8–10 µg | Micrograms |

# Recipe

### Lemon crust cake

150 g soft margarine
250 g caster sugar
150 g self-raising flour
2 beaten eggs
1 lemon

Heat oven to 180°C 350°F, gas mark 4.

Grease and line a Swiss roll tin.

Melt the margarine. Add 150 g of caster sugar, the flour and beaten eggs and mix together.

Put the mixture into the tin and bake for 25 minutes. The cake is cooked if it is 'springy' when pressed.

While the cake is cooking, grate the lemon rind very finely and squeeze out the juice.

Heat the rind, juice and the rest of the caster sugar gently. Do not boil.

Spread this mixture over the cake whilst it is still hot. Cool in the tin.

Remove from the tin and cut into one portion slices when cold.

### Note

This cake is best kept for a couple of days before eating. It becomes increasingly moist and will remain moist for at least ten days if kept in a cake tin. A thin slice is a delicious accompaniment to stewed fruit.

The recipe can be varied by substituting a lime or an orange for the lemon.

*Some and b*

## Structure

Meat is made up of:
- water
- protein
- fat.

Average lean meat muscle is:
- 76% water
- 20% protein
- 4% fat.

### Average composition of three different meats

|       | Water (%) | Protein (%) | Fat (%) |
|-------|-----------|-------------|---------|
| Beef  | 54        | 29          | 14.8    |
| Pork  | 56.5      | 27.5        | 16.1    |
| Lamb  | 51.2      | 25.6        | 21.6    |

The texture and taste of cooked meat depends on:
- the amount of water and fat in the meat
- the particular kinds of proteins in the meat.

## Muscle fibres

Carcass meat (i.e. the raw meat available in shops) is muscle with connective tissue, fat and gristle (i.e. white, tough tissue and cartilage). Muscle is made up of bundles of **muscle fibres**. Muscle fibres (sometimes called **myofibrils**) are very small tubes filled with water containing dissolved **muscle proteins** (**myosin** and **actin** are the most important) and **mineral salts**. Bundles of fibres can be seen with the naked eye and look like this:

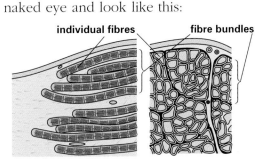

*Muscle fibres, shown lengthways (left) and in cross-section (right)*

Myosin and actin make it possible for the muscle to contract (i.e. shorten its length) and create movement in the body (e.g. as in running, walking, etc.).

**This is what happens:**
- The myosin and actin slide past each other, shortening the overall length of the muscle.
- They then lock into place.

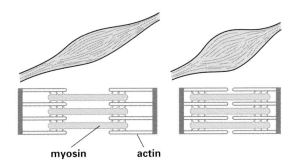

*The action of myosin and actin, contracting a muscle*

This information is useful because when there is a lot of movement in muscles the resulting carcass meat can be tough and needs careful cooking to make it tender.

## Connective tissue

Carcass meat has several types of connective tissue. One type, called **collagen**:
- surrounds the fibres to make a bundle
- wraps the bundles together to make the muscle
- lays a thin covering over the muscle called a sheath.

Two other types are **elastin** and **reticulin**. Elastin is contained mainly in blood vessel walls and the elastic **ligaments**, which attach the muscles to bone. It is yellow in raw meat and can stretch rather like elastic. Reticulin is contained in the spaces between the muscle cells.

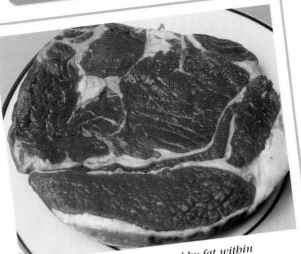

## Fat

Fat surrounds muscle tissue and is also contained within the muscle. It can be seen as flecks of white in raw lean meat. This effect is called 'marbling'.

## Colour

The red colour of raw meat is due to muscle cell pigment called **myoglobin** and to **haemoglobin** in the blood. Different meats vary in colour. Beef is usually darker than pork or lamb and meat from a young animal is usually lighter in colour than that from an older animal.

When the cut surface of any raw meat is exposed to oxygen in the air the colour changes to a brighter red. When left standing the meat changes colour again, this time to a browny red.

*The marbling in meat is caused by fat within the muscle*

lamb

beef

pork

*Different raw meats vary in colour*

**The tenderness and eating quality of meat depend on:**

- the amount and type of connective tissue
- the length and thickness of the fibres
- how much 'marbling' it has. This is important because when the fat melts during cooking it helps to separate the fibres, which makes the meat tender.

To make any cut of meat tender and ensure good eating quality it must be cooked by a method suited to its structure.

▶ **Beef** should look fresh and slightly moist. It should be smooth, with a fine texture and some marbling, and should not contain much connective tissue. The fat should be creamy white (darker in grass-fed animals) and dry.

▶ **Lamb** should be pinky red, moist and smooth. The fat should be hard and white and not too thick.

▶ **Pork** should be pink, dry and firm. The fat should be firm and white and the skin pliable and smooth.

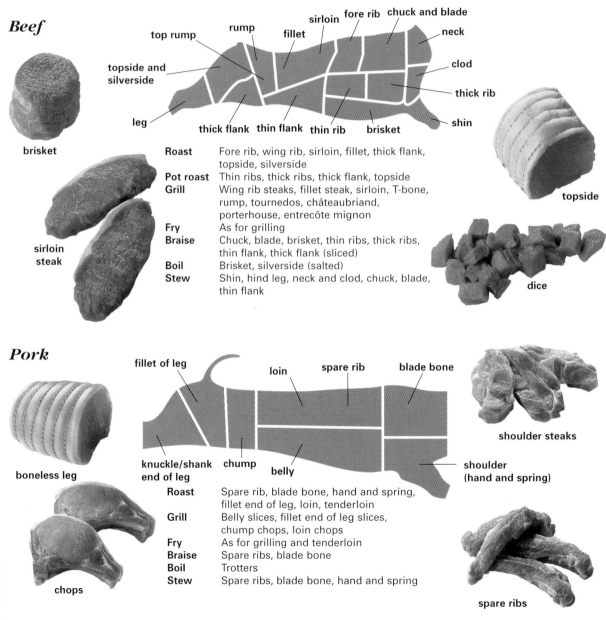

## *Beef*

brisket

sirloin steak

| Roast | Fore rib, wing rib, sirloin, fillet, thick flank, topside, silverside |
|---|---|
| Pot roast | Thin ribs, thick ribs, thick flank, topside |
| Grill | Wing rib steaks, fillet steak, sirloin, T-bone, rump, tournedos, châteaubriand, porterhouse, entrecôte mignon |
| Fry | As for grilling |
| Braise | Chuck, blade, brisket, thin ribs, thick ribs, thin flank, thick flank (sliced) |
| Boil | Brisket, silverside (salted) |
| Stew | Shin, hind leg, neck and clod, chuck, blade, thin flank |

topside

dice

## *Pork*

boneless leg

chops

| Roast | Spare rib, blade bone, hand and spring, fillet end of leg, loin, tenderloin |
|---|---|
| Grill | Belly slices, fillet end of leg slices, chump chops, loin chops |
| Fry | As for grilling and tenderloin |
| Braise | Spare ribs, blade bone |
| Boil | Trotters |
| Stew | Spare ribs, blade bone, hand and spring |

shoulder steaks

shoulder (hand and spring)

spare ribs

*Source: Meat and Livestock Commission*

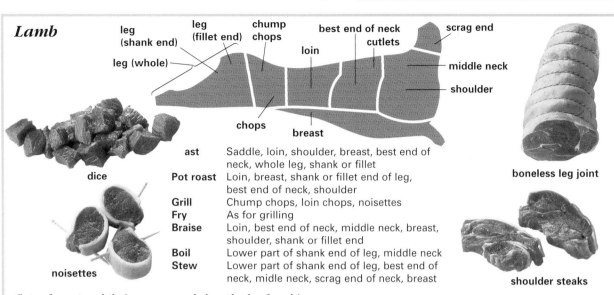

*Lamb*

leg (shank end) · leg (fillet end) · chump chops · loin · best end of neck cutlets · scrag end · middle neck · shoulder · leg (whole) · chops · breast

dice

noisettes

boneless leg joint

shoulder steaks

| | |
|---|---|
| ast | Saddle, loin, shoulder, breast, best end of neck, whole leg, shank or fillet |
| Pot roast | Loin, breast, shank or fillet end of leg, best end of neck, shoulder |
| Grill | Chump chops, loin chops, noisettes |
| Fry | As for grilling |
| Braise | Loin, best end of neck, middle neck, breast, shoulder, shank or fillet end |
| Boil | Lower part of shank end of leg, middle neck |
| Stew | Lower part of shank end of leg, best end of neck, midle neck, scrag end of neck, breast |

*Cuts of meat and their recommended methods of cooking*

## Health and safety

Raw meat may contain bacteria that could cause disease. Other bacteria can be passed on to meat during handling. Raw meat can be contaminated by faeces during slaughter, by unhygienic handling and by lack of knowledge about hygienic practices.

Provided the following points are remembered there should be no danger.

▶ Hands must be washed before and after handling raw meat.

▶ Raw meat must be stored and handled separately from any cooked foods. Any drips of blood from raw meat must not touch any other food. Any surface that the meat touches must be washed with very hot water.

▶ Raw meat should be stored and handled at low temperatures of 5°C or less.

▶ Meat must be covered when stored.

▶ Meat must be bought from a reputable dealer with a quick turnover.

▶ Meat that has been minced or cut into small pieces must be treated with special care, because the small pieces mean that more of the meat is exposed to contamination. Making smaller pieces creates a larger surface area.

▶ Most bacteria are destroyed by heat, so meat must be thoroughly cooked all the way through. Meat must be cooked long enough and at a temperature that will kill any bacteria (most bacteria are killed at around 60°C). The temperature inside the meat must reach between 70°C and 90°C. The meat thermometer below shows the temperatures which the centre of specific meat types should reach in order to be safe to eat. The use of a thermometer like this can help the cook check the temperature at the centre of a piece of meat. Frozen meat must be thawed thoroughly before cooking to make sure the inside temperature reaches this temperature range during cooking.

*A meat thermometer*

# Nutritional value

The chart below shows the nutritional value of beef, lamb and pork per 100 g. The nutritional value of 100 g of grilled bacon is included so that you can compare it with the nutritional value of the same quantity of pork. Bacon is produced from pork. If it is labelled 'smoked' it has been salted and heavily smoked; if it is labelled 'green' or 'unsmoked' it has only been salted.

**The nutritional value of beef, lamb and pork (per 100 g)**

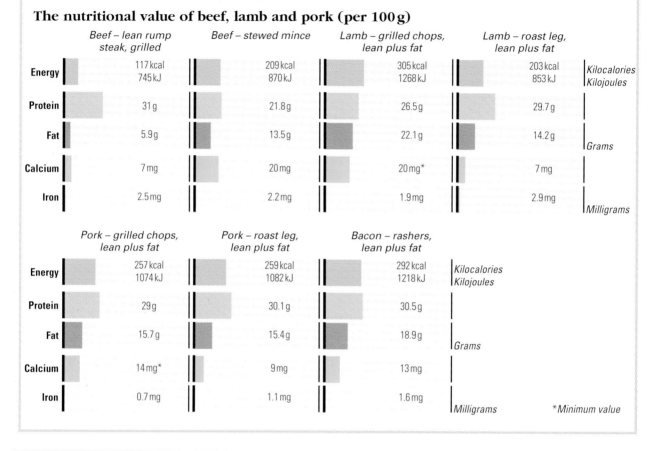

| | Beef – lean rump steak, grilled | Beef – stewed mince | Lamb – grilled chops, lean plus fat | Lamb – roast leg, lean plus fat | |
|---|---|---|---|---|---|
| Energy | 117 kcal / 745 kJ | 209 kcal / 870 kJ | 305 kcal / 1268 kJ | 203 kcal / 853 kJ | Kilocalories / Kilojoules |
| Protein | 31 g | 21.8 g | 26.5 g | 29.7 g | |
| Fat | 5.9 g | 13.5 g | 22.1 g | 14.2 g | Grams |
| Calcium | 7 mg | 20 mg | 20 mg* | 7 mg | |
| Iron | 2.5 mg | 2.2 mg | 1.9 mg | 2.9 mg | Milligrams |

| | Pork – grilled chops, lean plus fat | Pork – roast leg, lean plus fat | Bacon – rashers, lean plus fat | |
|---|---|---|---|---|
| Energy | 257 kcal / 1074 kJ | 259 kcal / 1082 kJ | 292 kcal / 1218 kJ | Kilocalories / Kilojoules |
| Protein | 29 g | 30.1 g | 30.5 g | |
| Fat | 15.7 g | 15.4 g | 18.9 g | Grams |
| Calcium | 14 mg* | 9 mg | 13 mg | |
| Iron | 0.7 mg | 1.1 mg | 1.6 mg | Milligrams |

*Minimum value

# Functional properties

The physical structure of meat determines its **texture** (i.e. the way it breaks down when chewed or cut with a knife).

## The effects of cooking on meat

### Critical points

- People expect cooked meat to be tender and juicy. Choosing an appropriate cooking method for a particular type and cut of meat should help because this will mean:
  - less liquid will be lost from the meat
  - collagen will be able to dissolve, which helps the meat to become tender
  - the meat fibres won't toughen.

### Proteins

- Meat proteins **coagulate** (harden) on heating.
- At around 60°C the proteins begin to change. This process is called **denaturation**, which means that the proteins change in appearance (their nature changes).
- As a result of denaturation:
  - muscle fibres become firmer
  - beyond 60°C the fibres shrink and the meat juices are squeezed out
  - water-soluble vitamins, mineral salts and the substances that give meat its taste dissolve in the meat juices.

## Dry heat or moist heat

▶ When the meat is cooked in dry heat (e.g. during grilling and roasting) the juices are lost from the surface of the meat. The 'taste' substances remain on the surface. This is why meat cooked by these methods has a very rich taste on the outside.

▶ Meat cuts with small amounts of connective tissue are the only ones that can be successfully cooked quickly at high temperatures in dry heat.

▶ Meat that is overcooked in dry heat is dry and tasteless because the muscle fibres shrink so much that all the juices are squeezed out.

▶ When meat is cooked in moist heat (e.g. stewing and braising) the squeezed out juices are collected in the cooking liquid. Cooking by this method produces moist meat with a good taste, unless it is overcooked, when it becomes dry, tasteless (because all the juices have escaped into the liquid) and 'stringy'.

▶ Collagen becomes water-soluble more easily when there is some liquid with the meat, therefore meat cuts which have a lot of collagen are best cooked by a moist heat method.

## Fat

▶ The fat on the outside and within the muscle fibres melts during cooking. This means that more of the collagen is exposed to the heat, which helps the meat to become tender. This is why 'marbling' is a desired quality in raw meat. A cut of meat that is not marbled (i.e. very lean meat) can be tough and dry when cooked.

## Colour

▶ The colour of meat changes during cooking because myoglobin becomes a grey brown. Colour is used to judge 'doneness'. For example, pinkness indicates underdone (or 'rare') meat.

▶ Another type of colour change occurs due to a particular type of browning. This is known as **non-enzymic browning** or the **Maillard reaction** (after the Frenchman who discovered it). This type of browning occurs in dry heat on the outside surface of meat when the carbohydrate and protein in meat react (work) with each other.

## Nutrients

▶ Nutrients dissolve in meat juices when they are 'squeezed out' during cooking as the muscle fibres contract. This means that the juices contain soluble mineral salts, vitamins and proteins.

▶ Some B vitamins (such as thiamin, folic acid and pantothenic acid) are destroyed by heat. For example, 30–50% of thiamin can be lost during cooking.

*Browning gives meat an attractive appearance*

# Changing the properties of meat

This is usually done to make meat have a good eating quality and 'mouth feel' (i.e. to make it more tender). Meat can be tenderized by **chemical action** or **mechanical action**.

## Chemical action

### Using acid

Mixing the meat with an acid such as lemon juice or vinegar before cooking, or by adding acids or tomatoes to the cooking liquid are examples of the use of chemical action. Meat can be soaked in, or painted with, a marinade before cooking.

### A typical marinade

Equal quantities of oil and either vinegar or lemon juice, a bouquet garni (bay leaf, thyme, black peppercorns, garlic and a piece of orange zest, tied together) and salt.

### Critical point

The acid changes some of the collagen to gelatin. This allows the meat to hold more water, which makes it more tender when cooked.

### Using fruit extracts

Extracts of fruits, such as pineapple, can be rubbed or painted on the surface of the meat. These extracts can be bought as granules, powder or liquid and are often called 'meat tenderizers'.

### Critical point

These extracts contain substances called enzymes. The enzymes partly digest the meat, which softens the muscle fibres and connective tissue.

## Mechanical action

Reducing the length of the muscle fibres improves the tenderness. This can be done by beating the meat to crush the fibres or by cutting it into small pieces such as cubes or mince.

# Combining meat with other ingredients

Certain types of meat can be made juicier and more flavoursome when combined with other ingredients, for example, extra fat. This can be added to very lean meat to make a juicy hamburger or beefburger. Similarly, flavours can be improved by mixing delicately flavoured meat with that of a stronger flavour, for example, minced pork mixed with minced beef in a meat loaf. Meat and vegetables are often combined to improve the flavour, for example in some stews and casseroles.

Meat is sometimes combined with other ingredients to reduce the cost of a dish, for example, breadcrumbs or textured vegetable protein (TVP) – see opposite. This is referred to as **bulking**. The added ingredient is used to extend or bulk out the product and reduce the overall cost.

# Other meat and meat-like products

## Meat products

These include burgers, luncheon meats, pâté and sausages, etc. Regulations cover the minimum meat content of these and similar products.

**Luncheon meat** must have not less than 80% meat, of which 65% must be lean meat.

**Hamburgers** must be made with either pork or beef or a mixture of these two. Not less than 80% of the ingredients must be meat and 65% of the meat must be lean.

**Pork sausages** must contain at least 65% meat with at least 50% of this being lean meat.

## Internal organs or offal

The word offal means 'off-fall' – i.e. the off-cuts from the carcass.

- Liver, kidneys and heart are the offal most usually eaten. Tongue, tripe (the stomach lining of cattle) sweetbreads (from the pancreas and the thymus gland) and brains are other internal organs used as food.

- Liver and kidneys have no muscle fibre or connective tissue. They can become dry and solid during cooking, so they should not be overcooked. Quick methods of cooking using a little oil or fat to prevent drying are best, e.g. frying.

- Heart is very muscular and dense (i.e. the muscles are very tightly packed). Slow methods of cooking (e.g. stewing) are best because it takes time for heat to reach the muscles and tenderize them.

## Mechanically recovered meat

This is meat that has undergone a mechanical process to remove meat fibres from the bone. These are difficult to remove by the normal methods used to cut up carcasses and remove meat muscle. The mechanical process makes sure that every scrap of meat is removed. A very small percentage of meat on sale is mechanically recovered, of this small amount 80% is from poultry, with the remaining 20% from lamb and pork.

## Meat analogues

These are 'meat-like' products.

- **Tofu** is made from ground and sieved soya beans. It is a soft semi-solid product and easily absorbs flavour from other ingredients.

- **Tempeh** is a fermented mass of soya beans. It is a solid, which can be sliced, flavoured and cooked in a number of ways.

- **Textured vegetable protein (TVP)** is made from bundles of extruded soya protein. (Extruded means that the soya has been made into a paste and pushed through tiny holes, similar to those on a mincing machine.) This produces chains of protein material which can then be flavoured in different ways.

- **Myco-protein** is produced by fermenting an organism (called fuscium graninearum) in a tank of water, maize syrup and nutrients. The myco-protein is chilled and then flavoured, formed into shape and cut according to the type of product to be made, e.g. burgers, sausages, etc. Myco-protein has a texture similar to meat.
  **Quorn** is a type of myco-protein. It is made from a fungus. It can be combined with sweet and savoury ingredients. Quorn is available in **ready meals** and as pieces of mince. Quorn is a trademark of its manufacturers, Marlow Foods Ltd.

## Fact file

### Tenderizing meat

Meat tenderizers can be bought in supermarkets and are used to make meat more tender. When using tenderizers remember the following points:

the tenderizer and the meat must be in contact (i.e. touching) for the tenderizer to work

if the tenderizer is put on the surface, only the surface will be tenderized

if the tenderizer and the meat are stirred/mixed together, more of the meat will become tender

if the tenderizer is left on the meat too long before cooking, the meat will become soft and 'mushy'

they work at warm temperatures (60–70°C) and stop working at higher temperatures. This is because the enzymes in meat tenderizers become denatured (i.e. they change their nature) at high temperatures.

## What is milk?

Milk is made from the water and nutrients that cows and other animals eat and drink. Cows' milk is the type most widely consumed in the UK. Other animals that provide milk for human consumption include goats and ewes (female sheep).

*Cows' milk is by far the most popular milk in the UK*

## Structure

Milk is made up of:
- water
- carbohydrate
- fat
- protein
- minerals
- vitamins.

0.7% minerals
0.8% vitamins
3.5% protein
3.8–5% fat
4.8% carbohydrate
85.2–86.4% water

*The average composition of cows' milk*

Milk is an emulsion. It has tiny drops of fat floating about (i.e. suspended) in a watery liquid. The watery liquid has proteins, milk sugar, vitamins and minerals dissolved in it.

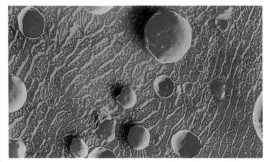

*Fat globules in whole milk*

The carbohydrate in milk is milk sugar, called **lactose**. Lactose has a slightly sweet taste, but is not as sweet as sucrose, the sugar that is sprinkled on drinks and food.

The main protein in milk is **casein**. Milk also contains small quantities of two other proteins – **lactalbumin** and **lactoglobin**. Milk separates into solid lumps called curds and whey when mixed with acid and/or **rennin**, which is an enzyme (see page 62). Enzymes speed up the effect of mixing one substance with another and are known as catalysts. Casein is sometimes called a curd protein because it forms curds. Lactalbumin and lactoglobin are sometimes called whey proteins because they remain dissolved in the liquid part of milk.

The most important mineral present in milk is **calcium**. There are also small quantities of **zinc**, **phosphorus** and **magnesium**.

All types of milk contain the water-soluble vitamins **riboflavin** (vitamin B2), **thiamin** (vitamin B1) and **nicotinic acid** (vitamin B3). The fat-soluble vitamins A and D are present in whole milk (i.e. milk from which no fat has been removed). Whole milk is a very good source of vitamin A. (See the nutritional chart on page 63.)

# *Quality*

Ninety-nine per cent of the milk sold in the UK is heat treated by one of three methods. It is either pasteurized, ultra heat treated, or sterilized.

**Pasteurized milk** is the most usual. It undergoes a mild heat treatment, which makes the milk safe to drink with hardly any change in flavour or nutritional value. It helps the milk keep for longer (i.e. it extends its shelf-life).

**Homogenized milk** is treated so that the fat droplets in it are made very small and are evenly spaced throughout the milk. This milk is the same throughout and does not have a cream layer on the top. The milk is forced through a very small nozzle at high speed and this breaks up the fat globules (droplets) to about a quarter of their original size. The milk is then heat treated. Bottles of homogenized milk have a red top.

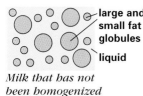

*Milk that has not been homogenized*

*Homogenized milk*

**Sterilized milk** is heated to at least 100°C for approximately 20 minutes. The milk tastes creamy and 'toffee like' and has a slightly reduced nutritional value because the heat destroys some of the nutrients, especially the B group vitamins. Unopened sterilized milk will keep for several months unrefrigerated, but it must be refrigerated and used within five days once opened. Whole, semi-skimmed and skimmed varieties are available.

**Ultra heat treated (UHT) milk** is sterilized homogenized milk, which is often packed in sterile conditions and heat-sealed in cartons. The cartons are made of a laminated material, which is made of layers of polyethylene, paper and plastic. Unopened cartons will keep for several months without refrigeration, but must be refrigerated and used within five days once opened.

**Dried milk** is a powder, made by removing the water from milk. The powder contains less than 5% moisture. The milk is homogenized, heat treated and then dried. The powder is packed in containers that keep air and moisture out. It will keep up to a year in a cool, dry cupboard. Once reconstituted (i.e. mixed with a liquid), it must be kept as carefully as fresh milk.

**Evaporated milk** is concentrated sterilized milk (i.e. the amount of liquid has been reduced by evaporation). The milk is reduced to roughly 50% of its original volume and is then homogenized to stop the fat separating out during storage. The milk is canned, sterilized and cooled.

**Sweetened condensed milk** is evaporated milk with added sugar. Sugar makes up 50% of the content, which helps to keep the milk safe (i.e. it preserves it). The milk does not need sterilizing during production. It is sold in cans and it can be made from whole, semi-skimmed or skimmed milk.

**Filled milk** is skimmed milk with added vegetable fat. There is a wide variety available, including dried filled milks. These can be reconstituted and used to replace fresh milk.

**Flavoured milks** are made from UHT or sterilized milk (mostly semi-skimmed or skimmed). Banana, strawberry and chocolate flavours are popular.

*Some of the many different kinds of milk*

Milk is perishable (i.e. it does not keep) unless it is sterilized or ultra heat treated and stored in containers which are not opened.

## Critical points

▶ Milk must be kept cool and covered.

▶ Storage places should be dark because light spoils the 'fresh' flavour and also destroys a lot of the riboflavin.

▶ Most bottles and cartons of fresh milk are stamped with a 'best before' date. This refers to how long it will stay in a good condition if kept in a refrigerator.

▶ UHT and sterilized milks have an extended shelf-life while unopened, but must be treated as fresh milk once opened.

▶ Clean containers must be used. It is best to keep the milk in its original container to store it, because these are sterilized during processing.

▶ Milk should not be left in a warm or sunny environment or it may become unsafe to use. It will also reduce the riboflavin and vitamin C content.

▶ Old and new milk must not be mixed together. It should be used in rotation – i.e. the older milk should be used up before starting the new milk.

▶ Reconstituted dried and evaporated milk etc. m

*Some more varieties of milk*

▶ Two of the milk proteins (lactalbumin and lactoglobin) coagulate on heating.

▶ When milk is heated and boils, a skin forms on the surface. The water on the surface turns into gas (i.e. it evaporates) and escapes into the air. Casein joins with the calcium in the milk and together they make a skin. If the milk is stirred or whisked a small foam is produced and a skin does not form.

▶ Casein does not coagulate unless the milk becomes acid. When milk is kept in a warm place for several days, bacteria change the lactose in the milk to **lactic acid**. This increases the acidity of the milk, which makes the casein coagulate. This is called **curdling**. If tomatoes, lemon juice or another acid ingredient are added, the same thing happens. Curdling can be avoided if the acid ingredients are mixed with a starchy ingredient (such as flour, cornflour, or arrowroot) before being combined with the milk. This 'holds' the casein in the liquid (i.e. it is held in suspension) and prevents a curd forming, i.e curdling doesn't occur.

▶ The enzyme rennin is present in the digestive juices of humans and cows and also makes casein coagulate. The enzyme is taken from cows to make a product called **rennet**. Rennet makes milk 'set'. Products such as cheese and junket are made using rennet. The casein coagulates and surrounds the liquid part of the milk to produce a set product. Rennet sets the milk when it is heated to blood heat only (about 38°C). The milk will not set if the temperature is too high.

▶ The functional properties of milk are altered by homogenization. For example:
   ◆ a rice pudding made with homogenized milk takes longer to cook than one made with non-homogenized milk. It is thought that the heat takes longer to pass through the pudding if homogenized milk is used
   ◆ in custards or sauces made with homogenized milk, some scientists have found that creamier, thicker (more viscous) results with good setting properties are produced.

# Nutritional value

It is important to understand that the amount of protein, calcium, carbohydrate and riboflavin (vitamin B2) found in milk is similar whatever the type chosen.

## The fat content of milk depends on:

- the breed of cow e.g. Channel Island breeds (Jersey or Guernsey) give milk with an average fat content of 4.9%
- the type of milk. For example, on average whole milk has 3.9% fat, semi-skimmed milk has 1.5–1.8% fat and skimmed milk has 0.1% fat.

The table shows:
- the nutritional value of different types of milk
- the similarities and differences between them.

## Critical points

- Protein is made of chains of small units called **amino acids**. The body can make some amino acids but it cannot make all of them. Those that the body cannot make must be supplied by food. These are called **indispensable amino acids**. The amino acids in the proteins in milk are indispensable, which is why they are so important.
- Milk contains no starch or dietary fibre, little iron or vitamin C but it is a valuable source of other nutrients.
- Most of the fat in milk is saturated fat.

## The nutritional value of various types of milk (per 100 ml)

| | Channel Islands | Whole | Semi-skimmed | Skimmed | |
|---|---|---|---|---|---|
| Energy | 81 kcal / 337 kJ | 68 kcal / 284 kJ | 49 kcal / 204 kJ | 34 kcal / 146 kJ | Kilocalories / Kilojoules |
| Protein | 3.7 g | 3.2 g | 3.4 g | 3.4 g | |
| Carbohydrate | 4.7 g | 4.7 g | 5 g | 5 g | |
| of which sugars: | 4.7 g | 4.7 g | 5 g | 5 g | |
| Fat | 5.2 g | 4 g | 1.7 g | 0.1 g | |
| of which saturates: | 3.4 g | 2.5 g | 1 g | 0.06 g | |
| monounsaturates: | 1.3 g | 1.1 g | 0.5 g | Trace | |
| polyunsaturates: | 0.1 g | 0.1 g | Trace | Trace | Grams |
| Sodium | 56 mg | 57 mg | 57 mg | 57 mg | |
| Thiamin | 0.04 mg† | 0.04 mg† | 0.04 mg† | 0.04 mg† | |
| Riboflavin | 0.20 mg* | 0.18 mg* | 0.19 mg* | 0.19 mg* | |
| Calcium | 134 mg | 119 mg | 122 mg | 124 mg | |
| Magnesium | 12 mg | 11 mg | 11 mg | 12 mg | |
| Phosphorus | 103 mg | 95 mg | 98 mg | 98 mg | |
| Zinc | 0.4 mg | 0.4 mg | 0.4 mg | 0.4 mg | Milligrams |
| Vitamin A | 60 µg* | 58 µg* | 24 µg* | 1 µg* | |
| Folic acid | 6 µg† | 6 µg† | 6 µg† | 6 µg† | |
| Vitamin B12 | 0.4 µg† | 0.4 µg† | 0.4 µg† | 0.4 µg† | |
| Biotin | 2 µg | 2 µg | 2.1 µg | 2.1 µg | |
| Vitamin D | 0.03 µg | 0.03 µg | 0.01 µg | Trace | Micrograms |

*will reduce if exposed to sunlight   † subject to degree of processing

## *Junket*

500 ml milk
1 tablespoon sugar
6 drops vanilla essence
1 teaspoon essence of rennet

Warm the milk and sugar in a saucepan to the heat of blood (i.e. 38°C). Test with either a thermometer or carefully with fingers. The milk should just feel warm.

Add the vanilla essence.

Pour into a serving bowl.

Stir in the rennet and leave for about 20 minutes, then put into the fridge.

Serve with slices of fresh fruit (e.g. banana) or stewed fruit (e.g. rhubarb).

Junket has an 'old fashioned' image but its smooth and set texture combines well with fruits. Use it as an alternative to yoghurt, fromage frais and crème fraiche.

## *Crispy refrigerator biscuits*

Serve with junket to provide a contrast in texture.

### You will need

1 teaspoon cooking oil
100 g softened (but not liquid) butter
50 g icing sugar
1 egg yolk
1 teaspoon vanilla essence
200 g plain flour
1 tablespoon caster sugar

### Method

Heat oven to 200°C 400°F, gas mark 6.
Grease a baking tray with the cooking oil.
Beat butter and icing sugar until soft and creamy.
Mix in egg yolk and vanilla essence.
Add flour and mix to a dough.
Roll into a sausage (5 cm × 10 cm).
Cut the dough into 3 mm slices and put on the baking tray.
Bake for 4–5 minutes.
Dust with the caster sugar whilst warm.

*The enzyme called rennet is taken from cows*

# Combining milk with other ingredients

There are nutritional advantages when milk is combined with other ingredients. For example, the overall protein quality is improved when it is served with cereals, or combined in dishes with nuts, pulses, cheese, eggs, etc.

Milk is an essential ingredient in batter, custards, sauces, drinks such as milkshake, egg flip, etc. For example, in batter sauces and cornflour custards, it is milk that combines with the starchy thickening agent (flour, cornflour or custard powder) and allows gelatinization to happen. The starch granules absorb the liquid, swell and soften when the mixture is cooled. In egg custards the milk combines with the eggs and causes them to coagulate into a soft and tender product when heated.

When milk is combined with fat, sugar and flour (as in a cake or scone mixture) it provides moisture which helps:
- the raising agent to produce carbon dioxide when heated
- to produce a tender crumb in the baked product. It does this by preventing the clumping together of starch and fat.

*Milk, fat, sugar, eggs and flour are the main ingredients of many products, such as pancakes*

# Fact file

As the United Kingdom is a member of the European Community, the rules of the Common Agricultural Policy (CAP) apply to dairy farmers in the UK. The CAP was set up to make sure that all the countries within the community should have sufficient supplies of food and also that farmers' incomes should be protected. Prices are prevented from falling and currently farmers are assured of being able to sell certain dairy products to the community (e.g. butter) if they cannot sell it to anyone else. This is called intervention.

The effect of this and higher prices in the European Community encouraged farmers in some of the member countries to produce a surplus of milk and dairy products. This did not occur in the UK. To try to prevent surplus production of milk a system of quotas was introduced. This restricted the amount of milk that could be produced in each EC country and now every dairy farm has its own milk quota. Any farmer who produces more than this quota can be fined (in fact for every extra litre of milk produced). If a farmer has a larger quota than he or she needs, the unused quota can be lent or leased for one year to someone who wants to produce more milk.

## What is poultry?

Poultry is the name given to the following birds, or 'fowl'.

- Chicken
- Duck
- Guinea fowl
- Turkey
- Goose
- Squab and pigeon.

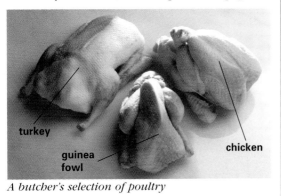

turkey

guinea fowl

chicken

*A butcher's selection of poultry*

## Structure

Poultry has a similar structure to other meats. It has muscle fibres and connective tissue. The muscle fibres are generally shorter which makes the meat more tender than, for example, beef or lamb.

The average composition of chicken is:
- 65% water
- 30% protein
- 5% fat.

The tenderness depends on the age of the bird and the amount of movement the muscle has had. So legs are always tougher than the breast, and an older bird is not as tender as a young bird.

## Quality

### Chicken

▷ Chicken can be bought whole or jointed (cut into thighs, wings and breasts).

▷ **Free-range** chickens have never been frozen. Their flesh tends to have more flavour because the chickens have been allowed to roam freely in the open air. They have not been kept in batteries or deep-litter houses.

▷ The feet, wing tips and breastbone of fresh chickens should be flexible (bendy).

▷ **Spring chickens** are about 8–12 weeks old. They are small birds weighing between 900 g and 1.5 kg. They tend to be tender enough to grill.

▷ **Capons** are neutered cockerels, weighing 2.5–5 kg. Neutering (caponizing) produces a bird with tender flesh.

▷ **Poussins** are very young chickens. A poussin weighs 500–800 g. It should have firm flesh and a good taste. One bird serves one person.

### Turkey

▷ Turkeys weigh anything from 3 kg–21 kg.

▷ Smaller birds are more tender and juicier than large birds, but have less flavour.

▷ Larger birds must be cooked very carefully with extra moisture, because the flesh tends to go dry.

▷ Fresh turkey should have firm white flesh, supple (bendy) feet and smooth legs.

▷ Female turkeys are more tender but male birds have more flavour.

### Duck

▷ Ducklings are young birds, weighing about 800 g–1.5 kg.

▷ Ducks are older birds and weigh 1–2.5 kg.

▷ The flesh is rich and fatty.

▷ Ducks are not as 'meaty' as chickens. There is usually only enough flesh on one duck to serve two people.

## Goose

▶ Geese are bigger birds, weighing 6–12 kg.

▶ Geese have very rich, dark and fatty flesh, which is usually tender.

▶ A good quality goose or duck has white skin, a plump breast and yellow feet.

## Guinea fowl

▶ This is similar to chicken.

▶ The flesh tends to be tougher than chicken. It is made more tender by being hung for two to three days before it has its feathers and innards removed.

## Squab and pigeon

▶ Squab is a young pigeon. It is normally about four weeks old and weighs 350–650 g. The flesh is tender.

▶ Pigeon is the older bird. Its flesh can be tough. It is best to remove the breasts and marinade them to tenderize them before cooking.

# Health and safety

▶ Poultry must be stored in the coolest part of the refrigerator. It must be frozen if it is to be kept longer than three to four days.

▶ Poultry can carry bacteria that can cause food poisoning (e.g. salmonellae, campylobacter, C. perfringens, and S. aureus).

▶ The giblets in fresh poultry must be removed before cooking.

▶ Raw poultry and cooked food must be stored and prepared separately because the bacteria from raw poultry can contaminate cooked food. The cooked food will not be cooked again, therefore the bacteria will not be killed and may multiply in the food.

▶ Surfaces and equipment used to prepare raw poultry must be thoroughly cleaned after use with very hot water to avoid cross-contamination.

▶ Poultry must be thoroughly cooked. Care must be taken to make sure the inside as well as the outside is completely cooked. The temperature must be high enough to destroy the bacteria (most bacteria are killed at around 60°C).

▶ Frozen poultry must be thoroughly thawed before cooking. If there is still some ice on the inside, the poultry will not be thoroughly cooked all the way through. The bacteria will not be destroyed and the poultry will be unsafe to eat.

▶ Poultry must be bought from a clean and reliable source.

# Nutritional value

**The nutritional value of poultry (per 100 g)**

The nutritional value of poultry is similar to other meats (see page 56) except for its fat content. This varies according to:
- ◆ the type of bird
- ◆ which parts of the bird are eaten.

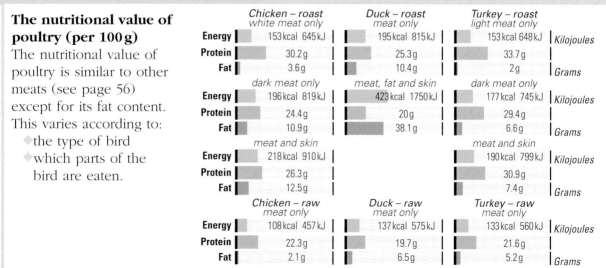

| | Chicken – roast white meat only | Duck – roast meat only | Turkey – roast light meat only | |
|---|---|---|---|---|
| Energy | 153 kcal 645 kJ | 195 kcal 815 kJ | 153 kcal 648 kJ | Kilojoules |
| Protein | 30.2 g | 25.3 g | 33.7 g | |
| Fat | 3.6 g | 10.4 g | 2 g | Grams |
| | dark meat only | meat, fat and skin | dark meat only | |
| Energy | 196 kcal 819 kJ | 423 kcal 1750 kJ | 177 kcal 745 kJ | Kilojoules |
| Protein | 24.4 g | 20 g | 29.4 g | |
| Fat | 10.9 g | 38.1 g | 6.6 g | Grams |
| | meat and skin | | meat and skin | |
| Energy | 218 kcal 910 kJ | | 190 kcal 799 kJ | Kilojoules |
| Protein | 26.3 g | | 30.9 g | |
| Fat | 12.5 g | | 7.4 g | Grams |
| | Chicken – raw meat only | Duck – raw meat only | Turkey – raw meat only | |
| Energy | 108 kcal 457 kJ | 137 kcal 575 kJ | 133 kcal 560 kJ | Kilojoules |
| Protein | 22.3 g | 19.7 g | 21.6 g | |
| Fat | 2.1 g | 6.5 g | 5.2 g | Grams |

# What is game?

These are animals or birds that are protected by game laws. They include:

- animals such as rabbits, hares and deer
- birds such as pheasants, partridges and grouse.

*Game hanging in a butcher's shop*

# Health and safety

- All game must be bought from a reliable source. Only those people who have a licence to sell game should offer it for sale.
- The smell should not be too strong or 'high'. The flesh should be firm and unblemished (e.g. no bruises, etc.).

# Structure

- The muscle fibres of all game are tough. This makes their flesh tougher than that of poultry, beef, sheep and pigs.
- Game creatures live a very active life. This accounts for the tough muscle and also means that there is less fat on the surface of their flesh.

# Quality

- All game must be hung for a period of time before it is prepared for cooking. This is to help enzymes in the flesh soften the muscle fibre so that it becomes more tender. The hanging time varies according to the type of game (e.g. venison, from deer, should be hung for up to 20 days or so, whereas rabbit should be hung for two or three days only).
- Fresh game is available at particular times of year. This is called the **season**. For example, the season for pheasant is from 1 October to 1 February. The season for venison is from August to September.

# Nutritional value

The nutritional value of game is similar to that of meat (see page 56) except for the fat content. All game is low in fat, but not as low in fat as chicken. For example:

**Amounts of fat in three types of game (per 100 g)**

| | roast venison (from deer) | stewed rabbit | roast pheasant | |
|---|---|---|---|---|
| Fat | 6.4g | 7.7g | 9.3g | Grams |

# Functional properties of poultry and game

- These are similar to meat such as beef, lamb, etc. (see page 56).
- The lack of fat on the surface of the flesh means the meat will dry out during dry methods of cooking. Extra fat should be placed on the outside surface to keep the flesh moist.

- Marinating in mixtures of beer or wine, oil, vinegar and herbs, etc. improves the taste and helps to tenderize the flesh. The acid ingredients in the marinade act on the tough muscle and soften it. The muscle tissue partly separates from some of the connective tissue. The heat can then reach the connective tissue more easily and convert it to gelatin.

# Combining poultry and game with other ingredients

## Poultry

▶Poultry can be made more flavoursome when combined with accompaniments such as sage and onion stuffing or parsley and thyme stuffing. The herbs and the onion have stronger flavours and provide a contrast with the delicate poultry taste. Curry and wine sauces are other examples.

▶Other ingredients provide the moisture which is sometimes lacking in poultry because of its low fat content. Examples include stock and vegetables (as in a casserole) or sauce (as in chicken fricassee). Poultry is sometimes combined with a 'casing' to keep it moist (e.g. chicken pasties, etc.).

▶A crispy texture can be produced, as in the egg and crumb coating used for Chicken Maryland.

*Chicken combines well with other ingredients to make many delicious dishes*

## Game

▶Game meat is sometimes combined with acid ingredients such as acidy fruit (e.g. blackcurrants). This helps to tenderize the meat. It also provides a contrasting taste, which complements the strong taste which most game meat has.

▶Game meat is also tenderized when it is soaked (marinated) before cooking. The most usual mixture is a combination of herbs and an acid ingredient such as fruit juice, vinegar, etc.

*Game can be combined with other ingredients to make tasty dishes*

# Recipe

## *Pear and ginger pheasant*

1 pheasant            50 g butter
3 peeled and sliced onions
4 cm piece fresh ginger cut into very thin slices
10 g plain flour
1 crushed clove of garlic
275 ml chicken stock
275 ml apple juice
salt and pepper
2 peeled and sliced conference pears

  Heat oven to 180°C 350°F, gas mark 4.

Melt the butter in an ovenproof casserole, add the pheasant and cook until brown. Remove the pheasant from the casserole. Cook the onions gently in the casserole until soft. Add the ginger, garlic and flour. Cook for about one minute.
Add the stock and apple juice. Bring to the boil, stirring. Add salt and pepper. Return the pheasant to the casserole. Cook in the oven for 30 minutes.
Add the pears. Cook for 30 minutes. Remove from the oven and put the pheasant on a serving dish.
Serve the onion, pear and ginger sauce separately.

# 14 SPICES

## What are spices?

▶ Spices are the dried flowers, seeds, leaves, bark and roots of aromatic plants.

▶ Most spices are available whole or ground (i.e. powdered).

▶ Spices were first used in cooking in China, India, and South-East Asia. The spices which grew in these areas were used to flavour ingredients which would otherwise be bland and uninteresting, such as rice, fish, poultry, etc.

▶ Spices have strong, pungent tastes and odours. These come from the **aromatic oils** present in them.

## Quality

▶ Spices do not have a long shelf-life, and quickly lose their ability to flavour foods. This means that they should be bought:
  ◆ in small quantities
  ◆ from a shop that sells a lot (has a large and quick turnover).

▶ Spices must be stored in airtight containers.

▶ Whole spices have more taste and odour than ground spices. This is because the aromatic oils disappear quickly when the spice is ground (i.e. the oils are volatile and evaporate into the air). Therefore, grinding spices just before use gives the strongest odour and taste.

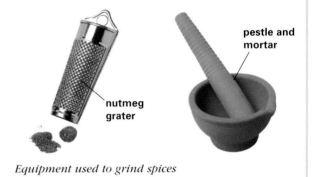

*Equipment used to grind spices*

## Functional properties of various spices

| Spice | What is it? | Functional properties |
|-------|-------------|------------------------|
| **Allspice** | The dried fruit of the pimento tree. | It is called allspice because it tastes like a mixture of nutmeg, cloves and cinnamon. It is used in baking, pickling and for flavouring some savoury products (e.g. red cabbage, pork stir-fry, etc.) |
| **Anise-pepper** (sometimes called Szechwan pepper) | This is the dried berry of a tree which grows in China. | It has a peppery taste. It is used in Chinese five-spice powder. |
| **Caraway** | This is the seed of a feathery European plant. | It has a strong liquorice taste and odour. It is popular in Jewish cooking. It is also used in soups, salads and baking, e.g. seed cake has caraway seeds in it. |
| **Cardamom** | This is the pod containing small black seeds of the plant. | The seeds smell strongly of camphor. They give rice, curry and some sweet dishes a scented odour. The pods should not be eaten; they should be removed from the product before it is served. |

| Spice | What is it? | Functional properties |
|---|---|---|
| **Cayenne pepper** | This is made from chilli pepper that comes from Cayenne in Africa. | It is extremely 'hot' and must be used in very small amounts. It brings out the flavour of other ingredients, e.g. cheese and some fish. It is bright red in colour and is used in tiny amounts to garnish savoury dishes. |
| **Chilli** There is a wide variety of chillies ranging from mild to very hot. | Chilli is available either as whole fresh red chillies, dried whole red chillies, ground red chillies or fresh green chillies. | They can be chopped and added to salad mixtures, e.g. as in salsas, or when ground they combine well with meat to make dishes such as chilli con carne. |
| **Chinese five-spice powder** | This is made from a number of spices blended together. | It produces a liquorice flavour and is used in many Chinese savoury dishes. |
| **Cinnamon** | This is the aromatic bark of a type of laurel tree. It is available as bark, a stick or ground into powder. | Cinnamon combines well with fruit (particularly apples), with rice, fish, chicken and ham dishes and with egg and milk dishes, such as custards. Ground cinnamon is combined with dried fruit in a fruit cake mixture. |
| **Cloves** | These are the hard dried flower buds of the clove tree. The buds are picked before they open and are then dried in the sun. | The essential oil they contain is very strong. It is sometimes dabbed on to a tooth to stop toothache. The bud is used in baking and pickling. |

chillies
cayenne pepper
cardamom
anise-pepper
allspice
cinammon sticks
cloves
caraway
Chinese five-spice powder

*The spices mentioned on these pages*

| Spice | What is it? | Functional properties |
|---|---|---|
| **Cumin** | This is rather like caraway seed. | It has a strong, 'savoury' taste. It combines well with meat and other spices to make curry. |
| **Fenugreek** | The name means 'Greek hay'. The seeds are available as a spice and the leaves as a herb. | It is used a great deal in curries. It has an 'earthy' taste. |
| **Ginger** | This is the root system (or rhizome) of a plant grown in South-East Asia. It is available whole, sliced or ground. Crystallized ginger is pieces of the root stem preserved in sugar. | All forms of ginger have a 'sharp' odour and a strong, hot taste. Pieces of ginger combine well with citrus fruits such as lime and lemon in mild curry mixtures. Ground ginger gives gingerbread and parkin their characteristic spicy flavour. In these mixtures the ground ginger combines with the sweetness of the treacle or syrup in the recipes. Ginger root and ground ginger are used in savoury dishes, such as stir-fry mixtures and curry. Pieces of ginger can be preserved in syrup and used in cakes and puddings. |
| **Mace and nutmeg** These both come from the evergreen myrtle tree, which grows in Indonesia. | Mace is the hard shell, which covers the nutmeg. The shell is peeled away, pressed flat and dried to form blades of mace. It is also available ground. Nutmeg is the 'nut' or dried seed of the fruit. It is available whole or ground. | Mace combines well with vinegar in pickles and with other ingredients in savoury dishes. Nutmeg gives the best results if grated or ground just before use. It combines well with milk and egg in sweet dishes such as milk puddings and custards. Both mace and nutmeg provide a similar flavour. |
| **Mustard seed** The word mustard comes from a Latin word which means 'burning must'. | There are a number of different types. They are all seeds of a plant. | Mustard seeds vary in taste from mild to very hot and are used to make different kinds of mustard. |
| **Paprika** | This is a bright red powder made from a variety of pepper that grows in South America. | The powder varies in taste between mildly hot to mildly sweet. It is used a lot in Hungarian cooking, for example, to make goulash. It combines well with meat, chicken and cheese. |
| **Pepper** | This is the dried berried fruit of the pepper plant. There are two kinds: **black pepper** (the berries or corns are greenish-black with a wrinkled skin) and **white pepper** (the same kind of berry or corn but without the skin). Both types are available whole or ground. | Black pepper has a stronger, 'hotter' taste than white pepper. Both types give better flavour if ground just before use. White pepper does not colour other ingredients, so it is best for white sauces, etc. |

| Spice | What is it? | Functional properties |
|---|---|---|
| **Poppy seed** | These are the seeds of the poppy. They are very small and black. | They have a spicy and sweetish taste and a hard texture. They are used in curries and for sprinkling on top of cakes and bread (particularly in Jewish cookery). |
| **Saffron** This is thought to be the most expensive spice in the world. | It is the dried stigmas of a particular crocus plant. It is available as whole 'strands' (stigmas) or ground. | It is used for colouring and flavouring cake and bread mixtures and rice dishes, such as risotto, paella, etc. It gives dishes a bright yellow colour and has a slightly bitter taste. |
| **Sesame seed** | There are a number of varieties. The ones most used are small, pearly-white seeds. They are the dried fruits of the sesame plant. | The seeds are crushed to make oil. They are also available whole. They have a nutty, slightly burnt taste. They are made into a paste called tahina and are also sprinkled on breads, cakes and salads, etc. |
| **Turmeric** | This is made from the dried root or rhizomes of a plant from the lily family. It is available whole or ground. | It is a cheap spice and can be used as a 'budget' alternative to saffron. It is a bright yellow colour and has a very spicy taste. It combines well with vinegar to make pickle, such as piccalilli. It is used in curry powder and as flavouring in savoury rice dishes. |

black pepper — — saffron

mustard seed — — poppy seed

sesame seed — — mace

turmeric — — ginger

fenugreek — — cumin

paprika — 

white pepper

*The spices mentioned on these pages*

# Fact file

## The history of curry

Thousands of years ago it was discovered that certain herbs and spices had properties which would preserve food. This was important in hot countries, such as the Indian sub-continent, Vietnam, Thailand, Malaysia and Sri Lanka, because the heat caused meat and other ingredients to spoil and decay very quickly.

Mixtures of herbs and spices were introduced as preservatives. The combinations of herbs and spices varied according to what grew well in a certain area. However, all the combinations were given the same name: curry.

# 15 SUGAR

## What is sugar?

Sugar cane

A sugar cane plantation

Sugar beet

A field of sugar beet

Sugar is made from **sugar cane** and **sugar beet**.

- Sugar cane grows in hot countries with a tropical climate (many hours of sunshine and lots of rain). It looks rather like a very tall grass when it is growing and can reach about 5 m in height.

- Sugar beet grows in countries with a temperate climate (i.e. seasons of warm and cold temperatures) – for example, the UK.

There are many varieties of sugar. They are identified by the size of the sugar crystals and by the colour.

- **Granulated sugar** is white. Crystals are the same size as those at the end of the refining process (see page 76). This is a general all-purpose sugar.

- **Caster sugar** is made from granulated sugar that is milled and sifted to make smaller crystals. The crystals are fine and white.

- **Icing sugar** is made from granulated sugar that is milled or pulverized to a fine white powder. The crystals are very small. An anti-caking agent (E554) is added to prevent the sugar going lumpy or solid.

- **Preserving sugar** is processed as granulated sugar, but the crystallization is modified during the refining process to produce a bigger crystal.

- **Cube sugar** is made from moist granulated sugar, which is put into moulds, dried and cut into cubes. This is usually white, but brown cube sugar is becoming popular.

- **Nibs** (uneven shapes) are a by-product of cube sugar.

- **Demerara** is made from **raw sugar**, treated with light coloured **molasses** or sugar syrup. The crystals are larger and coarser than granulated sugar. They are pale brown in colour.

- **Dark brown (Barbados) sugar** is small crystals of refined white sugar, treated with dark molasses.

- **Soft light brown sugar** is small crystals of refined white sugar treated with light coloured molasses.

- **Coffee sugar** is processed as granulated sugar, but crystallization is modified to make a bigger sugar crystal. These dissolve slowly in coffee, which means that the first few sips have a strong, unsweetened flavour. The coffee is gradually sweetened as the crystals dissolve. They are usually light brown. Many coffee lovers prefer this type because of the two distinctive flavours.

## Treacle and syrup

▶ **Black treacle** is made from molasses. It is a thick, heavy, dark coloured syrup with a strong flavour.

▶ **Golden syrup** is a refined, light syrup with a gold colour. Some of the sugar it contains is **invert sugar**. This is produced when sugar is heated with water and weak acid. The sugar (**sucrose**) splits into two simpler sugars (**glucose** and **fructose**) which, together, make invert sugar. Invert sugar is sweeter than sucrose, which is why golden syrup is very sweet.

*Different varieties of sugars and syrup*

## Cane sugar

The sugar is found in the soft fibre inside the cane. The canes are cut down (harvested) and taken to a sugar mill. They are cut, shredded and crushed and then mixed with water. This produces a sugar solution.

▶ The solution is boiled and mixed with an alkaline substance called **slaked lime** (calcium hydroxide $Ca(OH)_2$). This purifies the solution, by separating the liquid from impurities (which sink to the bottom or float on the surface).

▶ The lime and impurities are removed leaving a clear solution behind.

▶ The solution is heated until a mixture of sugar crystals and a liquid, 'the mother syrup', are produced. The mother syrup is molasses.

▶ The molasses and sugar crystals are separated by spinning the mixture very quickly in large drums. The drums have lots of holes in their sides. The molasses is forced through the holes by the rapid spinning (this is called **centrifugal action**) and the raw sugar is left behind. The raw sugar is taken to be processed at a sugar refinery. Molasses is used to make treacle and rum and some industrial products.

## Beet sugar

▶ Sugar beet stores its sugar in its roots. The beet is shredded and soaked in hot water to extract the sugar. The sugar 'diffuses' by moving through the cell walls into the water. The non-sugar solids are left behind.

▶ The sugar solution is treated with slaked lime ($Ca(OH)_2$) and carbon dioxide ($CO_2$) to remove impurities.

▶ The clear solution is then treated in a similar way to that of cane sugar until sugar crystals and molasses are produced. The raw sugar is then taken to be refined.

▶ Raw sugar, whether it is from cane or beet is sugar crystals coated with a layer of molasses.

▶ The molasses is removed and crystals of different sizes are produced during the refining process.

# Sugar refining

- Raw sugar is mixed with raw syrup to remove the outside coating of molasses. The molasses is 'spun off' in a centrifugal machine.
- The sugar is mixed with water, lime and carbon dioxide to remove impurities.
- The sugar syrup 'filters' through a bed of charcoal. The impurities stick to the charcoal and a clear sugar syrup collects at the bottom.
- The syrup is evaporated (to remove some of the water) to make a concentrated syrup (more strength, less volume).

- Sugar crystals are added. These are called **seed crystals**. The size of these crystals is the same as the crystals of sugar eventually to be produced. The seed crystals work by making identical crystals separate out from the syrup.
- The process continues until the crystals grow to the size of granulated sugar crystals.
- The remaining liquid and the crystals are separated by spinning in a centrifuge.
- The crystals are sprayed with water during spinning and then dried in a current of warm air.

*Inside a sugar refining plant*

## Health and safety

- Sugar becomes damp very easily so sugar of all types should be kept in an airy, dry place.
- Dry sugar (e.g. granulated and caster) has a very long shelf-life.
- Syrups and treacles also have a long shelf-life. But after about a year some of the water is lost (by evaporation). Some of the sugar then makes crystals and a grainy texture develops.

## Nutritional value

- Sugar is almost 100% carbohydrate.
- It has a high calorific value. It can produce a large quantity of energy quickly.

**The nutritional value of white sugar (per 100 g)**

| Energy | 394 kcal 1680 kJ | Kilocalories Kilojoules |
|---|---|---|
| Carbohydrate | 99.9 g | Grams |

- Brown sugar contains tiny traces of minerals but they are far too small to be nutritionally beneficial. The only difference between brown and white sugar is flavour.

# Functional properties

Sugar has a large number of characteristics that make it useful in food production.

## Sweetness

▶The sweet flavour of sugar is used to:
- reduce the acidy sharpness of food, for example when sprinkled on grapefruit or when added to stewed rhubarb
- improve the flavour of some foods. For example, the natural flavour of fruit is 'strengthened' (or enhanced) when sugar is added.
- sweeten a whole variety of drinks and products (e.g. coffee, tea, biscuits, cakes and some manufactured products such as baked beans and tomato sauce).

## Browning

▶Sugar helps to colour products. When it is heated in a liquid it begins to turn brown when the temperature reaches 154°C. This is called caramelization.

▶Other browning occurs when sugar and amino acids 'work' together (interact) in baked products. This is called **non-enzymic browning** or the **Maillard reaction** (after the French scientist who discovered it).

*Sugar solution is browned on top of crème brulée*

## Aeration

▶Sugar helps to make mixtures light and risen. This is called **aeration**. When sugar is added to fat and creamed, the crystals of sugar mix with the fat and the air which is beaten into the mixture sticks to the crystals. The fat surrounds the air bubbles and 'traps' them in the mixture. The large number of fine crystals in caster sugar give the best results. This is because more crystals mean that more air bubbles are produced in the mixture. (Note, however, that icing sugar crystals are much too small for this purpose, and do not work in the same way.)

## Texture/mouth feel

▶Sugar is attracted to water (i.e. it is **hygroscopic**). This property means that sugar helps products to remain moist. This keeps them in good condition for longer, so they have a longer shelf-life and the texture and mouth feel of the products are maintained for a longer time. Bread and cakes are examples of this. If treacle or a syrup, such as golden syrup, is included in a recipe, the type of sugar they contain (fructose) absorbs a lot of moisture from the atmosphere (i.e. it works as a **humectant**). Honey is also a humectant. This is why products made with golden syrup, treacle, honey, etc. (such as gingerbread, parkin, honey cake, etc.) keep moist and in good condition for a long time.

▶The water-attracting property of sugar also helps to make baked products tender. This is because the sugar takes up some of the water that would be taken up by the protein in flour. Gluten development is reduced and a more tender, soft crumb is produced as a result.

▶Sugar also helps to tenderize meat. It can be added to a marinade in which the meat soaks or it may be sprinkled on its surface.

# Coagulation

▶ Sugar increases the coagulation temperature of eggs and gluten in a mixture. This means that the gas cells in a mixture have more time to expand before the mixture sets, thus making a more risen, lighter result.

▶ Sugar helps to avoid curdling in products such as egg custards, because it raises the temperatures at which the egg proteins coagulate.

▶ Sugar also can decrease the thickness (viscosity) of starch-based puddings and sauces because it raises the temperature at which thickening takes place. The product becomes thinner on cooling.

# Fermentation

▶ Sugar speeds up the production of carbon dioxide (the fermentation process in bread making). A small amount of sugar provides food for the yeast and gets it working quickly. The yeast attacks the sugar and carbon dioxide is produced more quickly. If too much sugar is added the process slows down.

# Foaming

▶ Sugar helps foams such as meringues to remain stable. This means that the air beaten into the egg white is not easily lost. The foam is strengthened (**stabilized**) by the sugar, and can be piped or spread etc. without the air bubbles bursting.

# Non-enzymic browning

▶ Cut raw fruit (e.g. as in fruit salads) does not brown when mixed with sugar syrup. It protects the surface of the fruit from oxygen in the air and prevents enzymic browning occurring.

# Preservation

▶ Sugar solutions act as a **preservative** in products such as jam, jelly, chutney and marmalade. Sugar is also used as a preservative in the bottling and freezing of fruit.

▶ Very strong solutions of sugar in water can be produced. They are called high concentration or 'heavy' syrups. Organisms that spoil food, such as yeasts and moulds, cannot live in these heavy syrups. This is why they are used to lengthen the shelf-life of fruits, etc.

▶ Sugar solutions can be boiled to different temperatures to produce different properties. The different characteristics are used to produce a variety of products. The table shows the temperature at which various characteristics develop, and the uses made of them.

| Boiling temperature | Properties | Uses |
| --- | --- | --- |
| 104°C | large gloss | Jam, marmalade, jelly |
| 107°C | thread | Sugar syrups, some icings, Italian meringue |
| 115°C | soft ball | Fudge, fondants |
| 118–121°C | hard ball | Caramels, soft toffee, nougat |
| 138°C | crack | Toffee |
| 143–149°C | hard crack | Butterscotch, nut brittle, barley sugar, boiled sweets |
| 155–190°C | caramel | For lining dishes and moulds, for colouring sauces, soups, etc. |

*Examples of some of the many uses of sugar*

## Combining sugar with other ingredients

▶Brown sugar or demerara sugar can be combined with many ingredients to deepen the colour of products or to provide 'bite' on the top of them. For example, in rich fruit cakes the use of brown or demerara sugar makes the crumb of the cake brown. Also, when either brown or demerara sugars are sprinkled on the surface of a product which is then baked or grilled, a crisp, toffee-like topping results.

▶Fine sugar, such as caster sugar, combines with eggs and flour to make light, fatless cakes, e.g. Swiss Roll.

▶Icing sugar combined with egg white or water makes icings of different types (e.g. glacé, royal or fondant icing). It can also be sprinkled for decoration.

# HONEY

## What is honey?

- Honey is the oldest sweet substance used by people.

- There are many types available in jars or the wax combs in which bees store honey (see below). The consistency can be runny or thick, and the colours range from golden to dark brown.

- Most honey is named according to the flower from which the nectar was taken (e.g. clover, lavender, orange blossom, etc.).

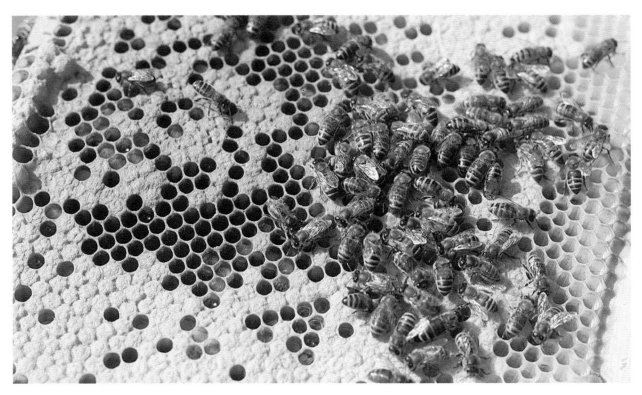

*A wax comb in which bees store their honey*

## Nutritional value

### The average nutritional value of honey (per 100 g)

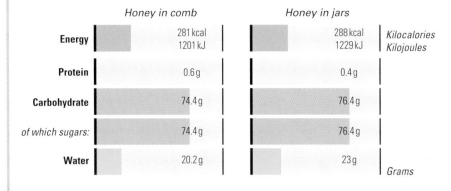

|  | Honey in comb | Honey in jars |  |
|---|---|---|---|
| Energy | 281 kcal<br>1201 kJ | 288 kcal<br>1229 kJ | Kilocalories<br>Kilojoules |
| Protein | 0.6 g | 0.4 g |  |
| Carbohydrate | 74.4 g | 76.4 g |  |
| of which sugars: | 74.4 g | 76.4 g |  |
| Water | 20.2 g | 23 g | Grams |

# Structure

▶ Honey is produced by bees from the **nectar** of flowers. The drawing shows the parts of a rose flower and a clover flower that produce (secrete) the nectar.

▶ Honey is a form of invert sugar (i.e. a mixture of glucose and fructose). The bees collect nectar from the flowers. The nectar is mostly sucrose and this is changed by a process called **inversion** into invert sugar. This happens as the nectar moves through the bee's body.

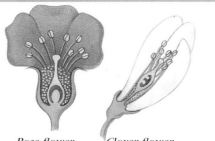

*Rose flower*    *Clover flower*

# Health and safety

Honey should be kept cool. It has a long shelf-life but will eventually harden and become 'grainy'. This is because, in time, the honey crystallizes. This varies according to the amount of glucose in the honey.

# Functional properties

Honey attracts water and keeps products moist. This makes it useful in baking. It also has a very appealing flavour.

# Combining honey with other ingredients

▶ Honey is excellent spread on bread.

▶ It combines well with lemon, as in a lemon and honey drink.

▶ It is combined with some breakfast cereals, usually as a coating.

▶ Sweet-sour mixtures for meat, fish, poultry, etc. can be made using honey as the 'sweet' ingredient.

▶ It combines with flour and fat to produce attractive baked goods, such as Turkish baklava (a type of flaky pastry with a honey and nut filling).

▶ It is used for curing ham. It can also be spread on the outside of ham, duck, etc. before cooking to make a crisp coating.

# Recipes

### Honey relish

4 level tablespoons runny honey
4 tablespoons tomato ketchup
4 tablespoons wine or tarragon vinegar
1 dessertspoon soya sauce

Mix all the ingredients together.
Store in a screw top jar or any container with a tight fitting lid.
Use as a marinade or as a sauce to be served with cooked meat, fish and poultry.

### Fudge icing

150 g icing sugar    25 g soft margarine
1 tablespoon milk    1 dessertspoon honey

Sift the icing sugar into a bowl.
Put all the other ingredients into a saucepan and heat gently. Do not boil.
Pour immediately into the sieved icing sugar and stir until smooth.
Use as icing or to sandwich cakes together.

# 16 VEGETABLES

## What are vegetables?

Some vegetables grow above ground; these include those whose:

- **fruits** and **seeds** are eaten – such as peas, beans, peppers, sweetcorn, tomatoes, cucumbers, marrows, courgettes, aubergines and lady's fingers (okra). Peas and beans are also known as **legumes** or **pulses**
- **flowers** are eaten – such as cauliflower and broccoli
- **leaves** are eaten – such as cabbage, Brussels sprouts, lettuce, spinach, watercress, chicory, spring greens, mustard and cress, Chinese leaves, etc.
- **stems** are eaten – such as celery, fennel and asparagus
- **shoots** are eaten – such as bamboo shoots.

Other vegetables grow under or below ground; these include those whose:

- **roots** are eaten – such as turnips, swede, parsnips, carrots, beetroot, salsify, radish, etc.
- **bulbs** are eaten – such as onions of all types, leeks and shallots
- **tubers** are eaten – such as potatoes*, sweet potatoes, yams and Jerusalem artichokes.

\* Note: potatoes are dealt with on pages 88–91.

## Structure

### Vegetable cells

- All vegetables are a collection of cells made of **cellulose**.
- The structure varies according to the type of vegetable and its age. For example, in leaves such as lettuce and spinach, etc. the cellulose is very thin. In 'old' vegetables the cellulose becomes thicker and a 'woody' material develops. This is called **lignin**, and makes the vegetables 'stringy' and tough.
- In between the cell walls there is a tough, insoluble material called **protopectin**. This cements the cells together. As vegetables ripen the protopectin becomes soluble (i.e. it dissolves). This produces a softer material called **pectin**.

The cells contain a lot of water, which keeps them rigid (firm). If water is lost, the cells become limp, flabby and lose their rigidity.

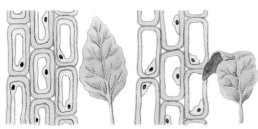

*The cells on the left are almost full of fluid, keeping the plant rigid. On the right the cells are almost empty and the plant tissue is weakened*

## Vegetable parts

Each part of a plant carries out a special job. For example, roots, tubers and bulbs are where the plant stores food. This is mainly sugar and **starch** with some vitamins (particularly vitamin C) and some minerals. When we eat roots, tubers and bulbs we are eating the plant's food store.

Leaves are where the plant builds up carbohydrate (starch) from water and carbon dioxide using energy from the sun. This process is called **photosynthesis**. In order to catch as much sunlight as possible the leaves must be spread out and be broad, flat and thin. Photosynthesis enables the starch to be carried to other areas of the plant. This makes the leaves low in energy value, but they are relatively high in some vitamins and minerals (e.g. see the nutritional value for cabbage in the table on page 86).

Fruits, seeds and flowers are where other plants store their food, in the form of starch and sugar. Seeds, such as beans, also store **protein**.

The part of the plant that is eaten varies according to the type of vegetable. For example, we eat the whole flower of a cauliflower, whereas for some vegetables only the seeds are eaten (e.g. peas are the seeds of the plant, removed from the pod in which they grow).

## Vegetable colours

The colour of a vegetable is part of its structure.

Green vegetables have a green pigment in cells within the plant. The pigment is called **chlorophyll**. The cells that hold chlorophyll are called **plastids** and are covered with a sheet (membrane) which allows water to pass through it to some extent. This means that they are **semi-permeable**. The chlorophyll loses some of its green colour when mixed with water, because the semi-permeable membrane becomes completely permeable and the colour leaks out into the water.

Red vegetables, such as beetroot, radish and red cabbage, have colour pigments dissolved in the cell sap. The pigments are called **anthocyanins**. They are very soluble and leak into cooking water.

Yellow and orange vegetables, such as carrots and tomatoes, have colour pigments called **carotenoids** in the plastids of the plant cell. They are **insoluble** in water and are not destroyed by heat. This is why carrots and tomatoes, etc. do not lose their colour when soaked in water or when cooked.

White vegetables, such as white cabbage and cauliflower, contain pale yellow pigments called **anthoxanthins**. These are **water-soluble**. The pale yellow colour changes to dark greyish brown when in contact with hot water for a long time (as when cauliflower is overcooked).

*A variety of cooked vegetables*

# Vegetable flavours

The flavour of vegetables comes from various substances in their structure:

- **Sugars**. Fresh, young vegetables taste the sweetest (e.g. 'young' peas). An exception is old carrots which taste sweeter than new ones.
- **Sulphurs**. The flavour of broccoli, Brussels sprouts, cauliflower, onions and leeks comes from the sulphurs in the vegetables. These affect the smell (odour) of these vegetables. For example, when onions and cabbage are cut up they give off a sharp odour. This is because cutting breaks the cells of the vegetables, allowing the enzymes and sulphur to mix together and produce the odour.
- **Acids**. All vegetables are acid.
- **Glutamic acid**. This is the amino acid that makes the flavour of young fresh vegetables so good.

# Quality

- All vegetables should be firm and have a good, bright colour when bought or picked.
- Damaged vegetables, for example wilted leaves and bruised flesh, will soon spoil (go bad).
- Vegetables are at their best when they are in season.

## Storing vegetables

- All vegetables should be stored in a cool, dark place. It should also be 'airy' (i.e. there should be air circulating around).
- Leaves, seeds and flowers (such as spinach, spring greens, peas and cauliflowers, etc.) should be kept in the 'crisper' drawer of the fridge. They should be eaten as soon as possible after picking or buying. They have a short shelf-life – two or three days at most.
- Roots, bulbs and tubers have a much longer shelf-life. They will keep for several months. Bulbs, such as onions, are best kept in a dry, airy place. Roots (such as carrots, swede, parsnips, etc.) should be kept in a dark, dry place. Sometimes when bought from supermarkets these vegetables are labelled 'store in the refrigerator'. Tubers, such as potatoes, must be kept in a dark place. If kept in the light they will sprout and turn green. Green parts of potato are unsafe to eat. See page 89 for information about storing new potatoes bought from a supermarket.
- Some vegetables are processed to give them a longer shelf-life. For example, by freezing, canning and drying.
  - **Freezing**. Examples include peas. Frozen peas are often of a better quality than fresh. This is because they are picked when young and quick-frozen immediately. They are given no time to spoil.
  - **Canning**. High temperatures are used to can vegetables. This softens the vegetables and means that all canned vegetables have a softer texture than fresh ones.
  - **Drying**. All moisture is removed from the vegetables when they are dried. They must be stored in a dry place. Peas, beans and lentils are examples.

## Pulses

These are seeds of plants called legumes. They grow in the pods of the plant. They can be fresh, frozen, canned or dried. There is a large variety available. Some of them have become fashionable. Aduki beans, black eyed beans and cannellini beans are all examples of pulses.

### Dried pulses

- These vary in appearance, texture and taste. They must be kept dry and out of the air (i.e. in an airtight container). They have a shelf-life of about six months.
- Lentils are one of the most popular dried pulses, particularly puy lentils, which are green.
- Other types of dried pulses include chickpeas. These are pale gold in colour and have a 'nutty' flavour.

## Baked beans

Baked beans are made from a type of haricot bean called the navy bean.
The diagram below shows the processes.

**1** Dried navy beans are checked and cleaned. Broken beans are removed. Then the beans are tipped into large metal storage bins called hoppers.

**2** The beans pass into a size checker which works like a giant sieve. Only the beans of the right size fall through the sieve.

**3** The beans are then 'blanched' – washed and soaked in hot water to soften them and make them edible.

**4** Clean, empty cans are filled with the blanched beans.

**5** To make the sauce, large rollers squeeze tomato paste into a tank where water and special spices are added.

**6** The sauce is heated with jets of steam, before being added to the cans.

**7** The cans are then sealed with lids and go through a machine called a cooker which cooks the beans at a very high temperature and then cools them straight afterwards.

**8** Hot air dries the cans so labels can be stuck on.

# Health and safety

- Dried red kidney beans contain substances that can cause severe food poisoning. The beans must be cooked at boiling point for 10 minutes to kill the harmful substances.
- All vegetables and salad ingredients must be thoroughly cleaned and washed before cooking. Soil must be removed because it can contain harmful micro-organisms.
- It is recommended that it is safer to peel all vegetables that may have been sprayed with pesticides.

# Nutritional value

Most people do not eat enough vegetables – they need to increase the amount they eat. It is recommended that everyone should eat five portions of vegetables (and fruit) per day.

## General points

- The energy value of most vegetables is low because they have a high water content.
- The protein content in most vegetables is low. Pulses, e.g. peas and beans, contain more protein than other vegetables.
- Unpeeled vegetables provide more dietary fibre than peeled ones (but see the recommendations in the 'Health and safety' section).
- Vitamin C is the main vitamin in vegetables. It dissolves in water and can be lost during cooking. (See 'Functional properties' for details about this.)

## The nutritional value of 100 g of various vegetables

|  | Beans (canned in tomato sauce) | Cabbage (green, boiled) | Carrots (old, boiled) | Peas (fresh or frozen, boiled) | Peas (canned, processed) | |
|---|---|---|---|---|---|---|
| Energy | 63 kcal 266 kJ | 15 kcal 66 kJ | 23 kcal 96 kJ | 49 kcal 208 kJ | 76 kcal 325 kJ | Kilocalories Kilojoules |
| Protein | 5.1 g | 1.7 g | 0.7 g | 5 g | 6.5 g | |
| Fat | 0.4 g | 0 g | 0 g | 0 g | 0 g | |
| Carbohydrate | 10.3 g | 2.3 g | 5.4 g | 7.7 g | 13.7 g | |
| Water | 74 g | 93 g | 90 g | 80 g | 72 g | Grams |
| Calcium | 45 mg | 38 mg | 48 mg | 13 mg | 27 mg | |
| Iron | 1.4 mg | 0.4 mg | 0.6 mg | 1.2 mg | 1.5 mg | |
| Vitamin C | 3 mg | 23 mg | 6 mg | 15 mg | 0 mg | |
| Thiamin | 0.07 mg | 0.03 mg | 0.06 mg | 0.25 mg | 0.1 mg | |
| Riboflavin | 0.05 mg | 0.03 mg | 0.05 mg | 0.11 mg | 0.04 mg | |
| Nicotinic acid equivalent | 1.4 mg | 0.5 mg | 0.7 mg | 2.3 mg | 1.4 mg | Milligrams |
| Vitamin A | 50 µg | 50 µg | 2000 µg | 50 µg | 67 µg | Micrograms |

# Functional properties

- When vegetables are cut, chopped or shredded, etc. the cell walls are broken. This allows an enzyme in the cells to mix with and destroy vitamin C. The enzyme is called **ascorbic acid oxydase**. It is destroyed by heat. To cut down the loss of vitamin C it is better to:

- keep vegetables as whole as possible; use a sharp knife to cut; do not chop or shred more than necessary
- cook vegetables immediately after preparing them
- put them into boiling water or hot fat to cook. This will destroy the enzyme and save more of the vitamin C
- avoid overcooking. The enzyme is quickly destroyed by heat.

Vitamin C leaks into water (it is water-soluble). This means that:
- as little water as possible should be used for cooking
- vegetables should not be soaked in water
- acids such as lemon juice will reduce the loss of vitamin C. However, acids should not be used with green vegetables because it causes them to lose their colour.

When the cell walls of fruit and vegetables are heated they soften. This happens because the heat weakens the cell walls and water leaks out of them. This makes fruit and vegetables tender. The water will continue to leak from the cells if cooking continues. This will overcook the fruit and vegetables and make them wilt and become 'flabby'.

## Combining vegetables with other ingredients

Varieties of different vegetables can be combined together to form the main part of a product, e.g. vegetable risotto or onion and courgette lasagne.

Vegetables such as onions, peppers, marrow, etc. can be combined with stuffings of different types to produce a dish with a particular taste (e.g. peppers stuffed with onion and garlic).

Combinations of cooked cold vegetables combine with sauces such as vinaigrette and mayonnaise to make varieties of salad (e.g. Waldorf Salad, Russian Salad, etc.).

Combinations of peas or beans with other ingredients such as bread and pasta increase the protein content of the dish. Beans on toast is an example. The protein from the beans complements the protein in the bread. This is known as **complementation**.

*Vegetables can be combined together or with other ingredients to make a variety of products*

## Fact file

Vegetables are grown all over the world and are now transported over long distances. Slight refrigeration is used to keep them in good condition as it slows down the ripening rate. Other methods include deep (quick) freezing. Crops such as peas and beans are grown especially for this method.

# POTATOES

## What are potatoes?

▶ There are a number of varieties. Some varieties are available at the beginning of the potato season, e.g in June and July. These are called new or early potatoes. Varieties include Arran Pilot, Home Guard and Pentland Javelin. Retailers often name the varieties of potato, so that consumers can become familiar with them.

▶ Second-earlies or 'mid-cropper' varieties are available soon afterwards (e.g. in August and September). These include Craigs Royal, Red Craigs Royal, Wilja and Home Guard.

▶ Main crop potatoes are harvested at the end of the season (e.g. in September and October) and are available right through to June of the following year. Varieties include Desirée, Maris Piper, Cara, King Edward, Pentland Crown, Romano Croft and Golden Wonder.

▶ There is also available now a variety of 'knobbly'-looking potatoes called Pink Fir Apple.

▶ Not all varieties of potatoes suit each cooking method. It is therefore best to choose the variety carefully. For example, earlies and second earlies have a firm, waxy type flesh which does not 'fall' apart. This means these potatoes keep their shape. However, they do not 'mash' or cream very successfully. The table shows which potatoes are best for which cooking method.

| Cooking method | Suitable varieties of potato |
| --- | --- |
| Salad | Arran Pilot, Pink Fir Apple, Golden Wonder, Desirée |
| Baking | King Edward, Maris Piper, Golden Wonder, Wilja |
| Mashed | Desirée, Golden Wonder, King Edward, Wilja |
| Frying (chips) | Majestic, Maris Piper, Croft |
| Boiling | Maris Piper, Epicure, Craig Royal, Wilja |

*Potatoes being harvested*

**King Edward**

**Pink Fir Apple**

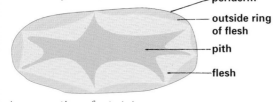

**Craig Royal**

**Majestic**

**Maris Piper**

*Varieties of potato are grown to suit different cooking methods*

## Structure

All varieties of potato have:
- **skin** (called the **periderm**)
- **flesh** (the area under the skin – this is fibrous and full of carbohydrate)
- **pith** (the innermost part – this is the watery core)

periderm
outside ring of flesh
pith
flesh

*A cross-section of a potato*

## Quality

The early and second earlies varieties should be used quickly. They do not keep, except in the case of Wilja, which will keep longer than the others. Main crop potatoes are bred to have a long shelf-life. If kept in their correct conditions they remain 'fresh' and good quality for many months.

## Health and safety

New potatoes should not be kept for more than two days. They must be kept in a dark, cool, dry, airy place. New potatoes are often labelled 'store in fridge' if bought prepacked from a supermarket.

Main crop potatoes that will keep longer must be free of sprouting. They must be dry.

Potatoes will sweat and rot in polythene bags. These should not be used for storing potatoes. Potatoes should be kept in racks or in paper bags, in a cool, dark, dry, airy place.

Even small amounts of light spoil potatoes by turning them green. The green must be removed before cooking because the green parts are toxic (i.e. they contain a poison).

# Nutritional value

In the UK, potatoes are a staple food and are eaten frequently as the main vegetable accompaniment to main meal dishes. The number of times they are eaten and the amount eaten by most people makes them a good source of vitamin C in the UK diet, even though they are not themselves rich sources of the vitamin.

## The nutritional value of 100g of potatoes cooked by a variety of methods

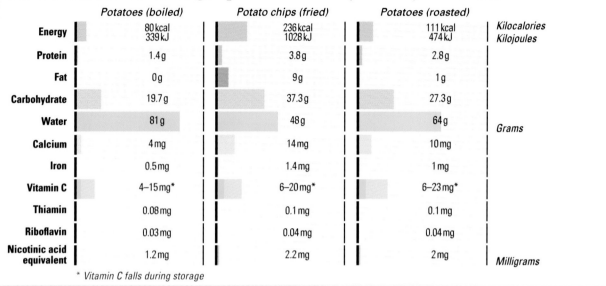

| | Potatoes (boiled) | Potato chips (fried) | Potatoes (roasted) | |
|---|---|---|---|---|
| Energy | 80 kcal 339 kJ | 236 kcal 1028 kJ | 111 kcal 474 kJ | Kilocalories Kilojoules |
| Protein | 1.4 g | 3.8 g | 2.8 g | |
| Fat | 0 g | 9 g | 1 g | |
| Carbohydrate | 19.7 g | 37.3 g | 27.3 g | |
| Water | 81 g | 48 g | 64 g | Grams |
| Calcium | 4 mg | 14 mg | 10 mg | |
| Iron | 0.5 mg | 1.4 mg | 1 mg | |
| Vitamin C | 4–15 mg* | 6–20 mg* | 6–23 mg* | |
| Thiamin | 0.08 mg | 0.1 mg | 0.1 mg | |
| Riboflavin | 0.03 mg | 0.04 mg | 0.04 mg | |
| Nicotinic acid equivalent | 1.2 mg | 2.2 mg | 2 mg | Milligrams |

*\* Vitamin C falls during storage*

# Functional properties

▌Depending on the variety, potatoes can be:
  ◆ granular and waxy
  ◆ floury or mealy
  ◆ sticky.

▌The cells of the potato change in different ways during cooking. If the cells separate from each other during cooking the cooked potato will be floury. If the cells 'stick' to each other during cooking the cooked potato will be waxy.

▌During cooking the potato starch grains absorb water. This makes them get bigger and they swell into a tender mass. The starch gelatinizes during the cooking period. If the potato is not cooked for long enough for all the starch to gelatinize, it will be hard in texture and taste 'starchy'.

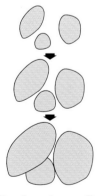

*Starch grains swell as they absorb water*

*Thicker chips have less surface area and so absorb less fat*

▌If the potato is cooked in fat, it absorbs the fat. The smaller the pieces of potato the more fat is absorbed. This is because the surface area exposed to the fat is larger. So thin, matchstick-type chips contain more fat than thick chips.

▌Potato starch makes an excellent thickening agent for soups, stews, etc. The starch absorbs the liquid, it gelatinizes and produces a gel which thickens the mixture. This gel does not break up if frozen and then thawed, so products thickened with potatoes can be frozen successfully.

## Combining potatoes with other ingredients

Potatoes are combined with most savoury ingredients, for example:

- creamed to make a topping for products such as shepherd's pie, fish pie, etc.
- sliced on top of a meat stew
- grated or creamed and mixed with egg batter to produce potato cakes and latkes

- boiled or mashed and mixed with fish, meat, nuts, etc. to make a cheaper product (e.g. fish cakes, rissoles, etc.). This is called **bulking** or extending a product
- mashed and mixed with flour and fat to make potato cakes, pastry, bread, etc.

*Potatoes can be successfully combined with most savoury ingredients*

## Recipes

### 'Red hot' potatoes

250 g new potatoes
(or Pink Fir Apple or Wilja)
1 clove crushed garlic
1 tablespoon olive oil
1 tablespoon tomato purée (paste)
1 level teaspoon paprika pepper
salt and pepper
1 teaspoon red wine vinegar
6 drops of hot chilli sauce or Tabasco sauce

Wash and scrub the potatoes. Cut into 'bite sized' pieces. Cook in boiling water until tender (about 15 minutes). Do not overcook.

Peel and crush garlic. Fry gently in the oil for 1–2 minutes. Remove from heat. Add all the remaining ingredients and mix. Drain the potatoes. Mix the garlic mixture with the potatoes.

Serve hot.

### Pesto mash

Boil and cream 400 g of potatoes to a mash with 1 tablespoon of hot milk and 50 g of butter. Add 1 tablespoon of 'bought' pesto sauce and 1 tablespoon of 'bought' tapenade.

## What is yoghurt?

- Yoghurt is made from milk.
- It belongs to a group of products called **fermented milks**.

- The milk of cows, ewes, goats and buffaloes is used. Most of the yoghurt made in the UK is from cows' milk.

## Structure

- The average composition of yoghurt is:
  - 86% water
  - 11–16% total milk solids
  - 3.5% fat when whole milk is used, 1–2% fat when semi-skimmed (partly skimmed) milk is used
  - 0.5–2% specially prepared starter (a mixture of bacteria)
  - vitamins and minerals.

- Yoghurt is grouped into **stirred** types or **set** types, according to how thick it is (i.e. its viscosity).

- The level of solids in milk has to be increased to make yoghurt. The percentage of total solids must be 11–16%. This is done by making the milk more concentrated, by evaporation, or by adding concentrated milk or skimmed milk solids. **Casein** and **whey** are the main proteins that are increased to make the total solids.

- The proteins coagulate and make the yoghurt firmer. This means the yoghurt is less likely to separate out during storage. A smooth texture and creamy flavour are produced as a result.

- The specially prepared starter for traditional yoghurt is called a **culture**. It is a mixture of equal quantities of Lactobacillus bulgaricus and Streptococcus thermophilus. These are bacteria that break down the protein in the milk during a period of time, called the **incubation period**.

- The bacteria produce acid and carbon dioxide in the milk.

- The **pH** of the mixture becomes more acidic (i.e. it is reduced to between 4.4 and 4.6). The production of **lactic acid** is partly responsible for this.

- The pH of yoghurt is critical. A low pH stops the growth of undesirable organisms but if the pH is too low (i.e. too acidic) consumers will not like the taste, as they prefer yoghurt with a pH of around 4.5.

- The starter culture for bio-yoghurt contains Lactobacillus acidopilus and Bitidobacterium bifidum in addition to the other bacteria.

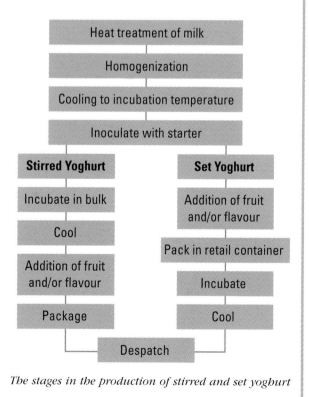

*The stages in the production of stirred and set yoghurt*

# Quality

There is a Code of Practice for the Composition and Labelling of Yoghurt. This recommends that:

- all yoghurt should have a minimum of 8.5% milk solids not fat
- all yoghurt should have a minimum of 3% milk protein content
- 'low fat' yoghurt should contain not less than 0.5% and not more than 2% fat
- the code also covers permitted added ingredients, such as preservatives, stabilizers, starch, colouring and flavouring.

Plain yoghurt should not contain preservative, thickener, colour or stabilizer. It should not be heat treated after fermentation.

*A wide variety of yoghurts is now available*

# Health and safety

Most yoghurt contains live bacteria so it must be stored chilled at a temperature of about 5°C. This gives yoghurt a shelf-life of about 14 days. Chilling:

- slows the activity of the starter culture
- prevents the yoghurt becoming too acid.

Yoghurt that is heat treated after fermentation may not contain live bacteria. It will be described as pasteurized, sterilized or UHT, depending on the heat treatment it has received.

All yoghurt will have a 'use by' date and should not be eaten after that date.

*Yoghurt should never be eaten after the 'use by' date*

# Functional properties

The thickness (viscosity) of yoghurt makes it ideal for 'holding' other ingredients together as in dips and cheesecakes, etc.

If yoghurt is boiled the viscosity is reduced. The liquid seeps out and a curdled mixture is produced.

If the yoghurt is mixed with cornflour before heating it does not curdle. The viscosity is stable to heat as the liquid is held in the mixture by the cornflour.

# Combining yoghurt with other ingredients

The most popular use of yoghurt is as an easily eaten, easily digested product on its own or with fruit.

The acidic flavour combines well with some spicy, savoury dishes such as goulash (a meat stew flavoured with paprika) or chilli con carne (meat flavoured with chilli pepper).

# Nutritional value

## Nutritional value of four types of yoghurt (per 100 ml)

| | Low fat, plain | Low fat, fruit | Whole milk, fruit | Low calorie, fruit | |
|---|---|---|---|---|---|
| Energy | 56 kcal / 239 kJ | 91 kcal / 386 kJ | 106 kcal / 447 kJ | 42 kcal / 177 kJ | Kilocalories / Kilojoules |
| Protein | 5 g | 4 g | 5 g | 4.2 g | |
| Carbohydrate | 7.3 g | 17.1 g | 15.4 g | 5.8 g | |
| of which sugars: | 7.3 g | 17.1 g | 15.4 g | 5.8 g | |
| Fat | 0.8 g | 0.7 g | 2.8 g | 0.2 g | |
| of which saturates: | 0.5 g | 0.4 g | 1.5 g | 0.1 g | |
| monounsaturates: | 0.2 g | 0.2 g | 0.8 g | 0.1 g | |
| polyunsaturates: | Trace | Trace | 0.2 g | Trace | Grams |
| Sodium | 83 mg | 64 mg | 82 mg | 73 mg | |
| Thiamin | 0.05 mg | 0.05 mg | 0.06 mg | 0.04 mg | |
| Riboflavin | 0.25 mg | 0.21 mg | 0.30 mg | 0.29 mg | |
| Calcium | 190 mg | 150 mg | 160 mg | 130 mg | |
| Magnesium | 19 mg | 15 mg | 16 mg | 13 mg | |
| Phosphorus | 160 mg | 120 mg | 130 mg | 110 mg | |
| Zinc | 0.6 mg | 0.5 mg | 0.5 mg | 0.4 mg | Milligrams |
| Vitamin A | 9 µg | 11 µg | 42 µg | Trace | |
| Folic acid | 17 µg | 16 µg | 10 µg | 8 µg | |
| Vitamin B12 | 0.2 µg | 0.2 µg | 0.2 µg | (0.2 µg) | |
| Biotin | 2.9 µg | 2.3 µg | 2 µg | N/A | |
| Vitamin D | 0.01 µg | (0.01 µg) | (0.04 µg) | Trace | Micrograms |

( ) estimated values
N/A value is not available

# Recipe

## Yoghurt dip

Small pieces of raw carrot, broccoli, cauliflower and other raw vegetables go well with this dip.

1 small carton low fat plain yoghurt
1 teaspoon red wine vinegar
2 tablespoons chopped spring onions
1 teaspoon mild mustard (e.g. Dijon)
salt and pepper

Combine all the ingredients together in a blender or food processor and liquidize until smooth.

Transfer to a small serving bowl, place in the centre of a large plate, surrounded by 'bite-size' pieces of raw vegetables.

This is a very healthy snack as the low fat yoghurt contains virtually no fat and is a good source of calcium, and the raw vegetables are full of vitamin C. Use this idea as an alternative to fatty or sugary snacks such as doughnuts and crisps.

# INDEX

## A
actin   52
albumen   32
amino acids   12, 19, 63
annatto   50
anthocyanins   83
anthoxanthins   83
anti-splattering agents   50
aromatic oils   70
arrowroot   15, 62
ascorbic acid oxydase   44, 86

## B
bulgur   14
Butter Regulation 1966   5

## C
CAP   65
capon   66
carotene   50
carotenoids   83
casein   19, 60, 62, 92
chlorophyll   83
clarified butter   7
coagulation   31, 32
collagen   52
couscous   14
crystalline fat   5

## D
durum wheat   12

## E
elastin   52
emulsification   31
emulsifying agents   50
endosperm   9
enrobing   39
extraction rate   9
extrusion   12

## F
fatty acids   22
fishcake   39
foaming   29, 31, 32
free fat   5
fructose   75

## G
ghee   6
gliadins   9
glucose   75
gluten   9
glutenins   9
glycerol   6, 22
golden syrup   75
ground nut   22
guinea fowl   66, 67

## H
haemoglobin   53
haggis   14
hydrogenation   50

## I
invert sugar   75

## J
junket   64

## L
lactalbumin   60, 62
lactic acid   62, 92
lactic butter   5
lactoglobin   60, 62
lactose   60
lecithin   31
legumes   82
lignin   82

## M
Maillard reaction   57, 77
marinade   58
mayonnaise   31, 33
melting point   6
myco-protein   59
myofibrils   52
myoglobin   53, 57
myosin   52

## N
non-enzymic browning   57, 77
noodles   14

## O
okra   82

## P
pectin   82
phenols   44
photosynthesis   83
pigeon   66, 67
polenta   15
proteolytic enzymes   45
protopectin   82
pumpernickel   14

## Q
Quorn   59

## R
reducing agent   44
rennet   62, 64
rennin   60, 62
reticulin   52
Ryvita   14

## S
sago   15
shortbread   7
slaked lime   75
smoke point   6, 25
soya   22
squab   66, 67
strong wheat   9
sucrose   75
sugar beet   74
sugar cane   74
sweet cream butter   5

## T
tapioca   15
tempeh   59
textured vegetable protein (TVP)
   58, 59
tofu   59
treacle   75

## V
vitamin C   44, 45

## W
wheat   9

First published in Great Britain by Heinemann Library,
Halley Court, Jordan Hill, Oxford OX2 8EJ,
a division of Reed Educational & Professional Publishing Ltd.

OXFORD MELBOURNE AUCKLAND IBADAN
JOHANNESBURG GABORONE PORTSMOUTH NH (USA)
CHICAGO BLANTYRE

First published 1998

03
10 9 8 7 6 5 4 3

**British Library Cataloguing in Publication Data**
Barnett, Anne
1. Food – Composition – Juvenile literature
2. Food – Analysis – Juvenile literature
I. Title
664'.01

Hardback ISBN 0 431 04894 0
Paperback ISBN 0 431 04895 9

Designed and typeset by Ken Vail Graphic Design, Cambridge
Cover design by Sarah Garbett
Cover photo by Haddon Davies
Illustrations by Barry Atkinson, Linda Rogers Associates
(Sara Silcock), Nick Hawken and Ken Vail Graphic Design
(Andrew Sharpe)
Printed in Hong Kong by Wing King Tong

## Acknowledgements

The author would like to thank Becky Pointer, for secretarial
support and unstinting use of her time and expertise;
Roy Ballam; Stephanie Valentine; James Garner and
colleagues; Dr Wynnie Chan; Dr Judy Buttress; The staff of
the Education department of The Dairy Council;
Shirley Ascough and the Meat and Livestock Commision;
Amanda Wynne; Barry Roberts and many others.

The publishers would like to thank the following for
permission to reproduce copyright material.

Meat and Livestock Commission for the material from their
meat poster on pp. 54–5; The Royal Society of Chemistry for
the tables from *The Composition of Foods*, McCance and
Widdowson, 5th ed. 1991 and its supplements *Meat, Poultry
and Game*, 1995, *Meat Products and Dishes*, 1996, *Vegetable
Dishes*, 1992, *Cereals and Cereal Products*, 1988, *Milk
Products and Eggs*, 1989, *Fruit and Nuts*, 1992, *Fish and Fish
Products*, 1993, *Vegetables, Herbs and Spices*, 1993, on pp.
10, 13, 19, 23, 28, 31, 36, 43, 51, 56, 63, 67, 68, 76, 80, 86,
94. Crown copyright is reproduced with the permission of
the Controller of Her Majesty's Stationery Office.

The publishers would like to thank the following for
permission to use photographs:

Birds Eye Walls, p. 39 (fishfingers); Gareth Boden, pp. 6, 7, 9,
10, 12 (pasta combined with other ingredients), 13, 14, 15, 17,
21, 23, 25, 27, 34, 35, 37, 39 (fishcakes), 40, 42, 44, 45, 47, 49,
51, 53, 58, 61, 62, 69 (chicken dishes), 70, 71, 73, 75, 79, 83,
87, 91, 93; British Potato Council, p. 88; British Potato
Council/NIAB, p. 89; Corbis, pp. 74 (sugar beet), 76; Farmer's
Weekly, pp. 74 (field of sugar beet), 80; Food Features, pp. 12
(pasta shapes), 38, 41, 57, 65, 66, 68, 69 (game dish), 74
(sugar cane), 77; Haddon Davies, pp. 31, 32, 33; Meat and
Livestock Commission, pp. 54, 55; National Dairy Council, pp.
60, 64; Sainsbury's, p. 18; Travel Ink/Colin Smale, pp. 50, 74
(sugar cane plantation).